THE
JESUS
CREED

loving God, loving others

for students

loving God, loving others

THE JESUS CREED

for
students

SCOT MCKNIGHT

WITH CHRIS FOLMSBEE AND SYLER THOMAS

PARACLETE PRESS

BREWSTER, MASSACHUSETTS

The Jesus Creed for Students: Loving God, Loving Others

2011 First printing

ISBN 978-1-55725-883-0

Library of Congress Cataloging-in-Publication Data
McKnight, Scot.
   The Jesus creed for students : loving God, loving others / Scot
McKnight with Syler Thomas and Chris Folmsbee.
      p. cm.
   Includes bibliographical references.
   ISBN 978-1-55725-883-0 (pbk.)
   1. Christian life—Catholic authors. 2. Catholic youth—Religious
life. I. Thomas, Syler. II. Folmsbee, Chris. III. Title.
   BX2350.3.M38 2011
   248.8'3088282—dc22

                                        2011003058
10 9 8 7 6 5 4 3 2 1

Published by Paraclete Press
Brewster, Massachusetts
www.paracletepress.com
Printed in the United States of America

contents

just a few words before we get started

First things first: this book is about following Jesus. Plain and simple. But before you take the adventure of learning what it looks like to follow Jesus, we urge you to pause and think about how to read a book like this.

The subject of this book is about the most serious topic one can imagine. *The Jesus Creed for Students* is about what it means to live a life now before God. It is about the revolutionary vision Jesus has for this world. It is a message that would turn local churches and communities upside down. But there's no secret here: this isn't a book about something that no one has ever heard. It is instead a book that draws our attention to Jesus. Sometimes starting all over again leads us to think we've never been there before.

We would urge you to read this book alone, all by yourself, in your room or in a quiet corner of a library or in a coffee shop. But the message of Jesus isn't to be kept to yourself, so we also want you to take another step: discuss this book with a friend, or more than one friend. Perhaps you want to discuss with your siblings or your parents what you learn and what you discover and what you are pondering. Maybe, too, you will want to sit down with your pastor or your youth leader and discuss what you are discovering.

Out of this process of reading and discussing, the next step is to begin comparing what Jesus teaches with what you are seeing in yourself and in your world and in your church and among your friends and in your family. Maybe you will see things about your school or in your community that call for fresh attention. This is where the message of Jesus begins to become revolutionary. But it doesn't become revolutionary by getting the world around you to change. It can only become revolutionary if *you* begin to practice what Jesus is calling *you* to do and to be and to live out in fresh, new ways.

What this book will do, we hope, is give you a new imagination, a sudden ability to dream of what you and your friends and your church group and your school and your community—even your country—can become if we learn to live out Jesus' incredible vision for this world.

Note: When the word *I* or *me* or *we* or *our* is used in this book, it refers to one of the three authors or all the three of us at once. Scot McKnight wrote the first draft, but both Syler Thomas and Chris Folmsbee hammered away at ideas, added comments, made suggestions for revisions, and even said, "This won't work." So the book in your hands is the *I* of three different people who are saying the same thing.

Flip to the back of the book if you'd like to read brief bios about each of us.

the Jesus Creed

Imagine Jesus standing in Jerusalem in the temple courts talking to a few people. If you don't have any idea what that ancient massive temple looked like, imagine Jesus sitting on the top steps of the Supreme Court building in Washington, DC, or holding court inside the West Wing of the White House.

Imagine now a religious expert, who has been sent by an unhappy and suspicious-of-Jesus group of religious experts, approaching Jesus in the temple.

Imagine the religious expert asking Jesus a question, a question that is aimed at Jesus for one reason: to trap him.

You need to know two things: the man's question was loaded with political implications, and Jesus' future hinged on his answer. Here's what the religious expert asked:

Of all the commandments, which is the most important?

The religious expert's question put Jesus in a politically vulnerable and religiously charged context. At that time there were serious debates between leading theologians about how to read the Torah (the first five books of Old Testament, often called the "Law"). Should it be simplified down to a few principles or should it be clarified into even more commands? If Jesus went in the reduce-it-to-a-few-principles direction, he'd align himself with the liberals. If he went with the make-more-rules approach, he'd line up with the conservatives. If he did neither, he'd offend both and look lame. What made the situation even more tense was that the religious expert was not really looking for information. He was trying to get Jesus in trouble by getting Jesus to take a position and offend one of the parties.

Jesus' answer baffled the expert. But before we get to his answer, we need to sketch what was going on in Jesus' world when the expert asked Jesus that specific question.

There's an old Jewish rabbinic story that a potential convert approached the leading conservative rabbi named Shammai and rather shamelessly said this: "Make me a convert, on condition that you teach me the whole Torah while I stand on one foot." This was a way of saying, "Reduce the Torah to a few principles so I can know if I want to commit or not." In your world, he was saying this: "Give me the *Spark Notes* version!" Shammai was offended by the would-be convert's irreverence and wacked him with a piece of wood and sent him away.

So the inquiring man went to a different school to find the more liberal rabbi Hillel and made the same request: "Teach me the whole Torah as I stand on one foot." Hillel, in a way that reduces the whole Torah to one firm handle, said, "What is hateful to you, do not do to your neighbor. That is the whole Torah. The rest is just commentary [on that command]. Go and learn this."[1]

● ● ●

This convert wannabe asked that question because there were many in the world of Jesus who were *adding commands*, and it was hard for him to know how to live before God. What do I mean by "adding commands"? There are, to be exact, 613 commandments in the Old Testament, one of which is "Don't work on the Sabbath!" But that raises this question: "What counts as work?" The "adding" group spelled it out and came up with a list of forty different activities that counted as work. So the one command had become forty commands. The result of the adding approach to the Torah was the multiplication of commands.

So you can see why the question was loaded. If Jesus decided to reduce the Torah as did Hillel, he'd get the pro-Shammai folks irritated. If he reduced it in a way that the pro-Hillel group didn't like, he'd irritate them. If he refused to play their game, he'd get everybody irritated. So, what did Jesus say?

Before we get there, what would you say if someone came to you and in a Snow-White-like question asked, "What is the fairest commandment of them all?" What Jesus said teaches everyone who wants to be his follower exactly how to orient every moment of every day:

● ● ● ● ●

What's the "fairest"
commandment of them all?

● ● ● ● ●

Part A

Jesus replied: "'Love the Lord your God with all your heart and with all your soul and with all your mind.' This is the first and greatest commandment."

Part B

"And the second is like it: 'Love your neighbor as yourself.'
All the Law and the Prophets hang on these two commandments."

Matthew 22:37–40

The whole Torah, not just part of it but the whole thing from Genesis to Malachi,[*] will be done if every day we love God with every molecule and globule (that's my translation) and love others as we love ourselves. Go ahead, Jesus is saying, read the whole Old Testament, and everything God tells you is either a love-God or a love-others-as-yourself command. (I suggest you sometime sit down with Exodus chapters 19 through 24, for instance, and in the margins mark "G" for love God commands or "O" for love-others-as-yourself commands. I've done this, and it works.)

How to keep this in mind

I call this love-God and love-others statement of Jesus the *Jesus Creed*. The Jesus Creed is the very core of what Jesus wanted his disciples to practice. At the time of Jesus, every faithful Jew began and ended his or her day by reciting what is called the *Shema*,[†] and the *Shema* is part A above. It can be found in Deuteronomy chapter 6, verses 4 and 5 (and one can extend it to verse 9). Every time observant Jews walked out the door of their home or entered the door of their home, they said it again. Not only that, but if they were walking on the path with their children, they were to say the *Shema* again to teach their children how to live.

So, when Jesus begins his "what's the fairest of them all?" answer, he recites something he's been reciting since he learned to speak. He would have learned to recite the *Shema* from his earthly father, Joseph, and his mother, Mary.

But Jesus goes beyond this: he *adds* to the sacred *Shema* another command, the love-others command. He picked this from Leviticus, what my students sometimes call the "Bible's weird book" because of its in-our-world strange purity codes. Anyway, by adding from Leviticus

---

[*] The Bible at the time of Jesus was organized differently from yours. The Torah was followed by the Prophets (from Joshua to Malachi) and then the Writings (Job and Psalms and Proverbs, but the Writings ended with 1–2 Chronicles).

[†] Please do not pronounce the Hebrew word *Shema* like this: "Sheee-mah." Say it like this: "Sh'ma." That is, with a very quick and almost silent "e."

the love-others command to the love-God command, Jesus gave to his followers a brand new form of the *Shema*. Instead of calling this the Jesus *Shema*, I call it the Jesus Creed. It is Jesus' version of the *Shema*.

Everything after this page will be shaped by the Jesus Creed. If Jesus thought the whole of God's will for us is to love God and to love others, then everything he calls us to be and to do is related to the Jesus Creed.

Now my suggestion
I suggest you try this for one month.

- When you get up, say the Jesus Creed (memorize the words in italics on page 11 or look at the end of this book where it is found along with the Lord's Prayer).
- When you go to bed, say it again.
- When you leave your house, say it again. When you enter your house, say it one more time.
- Then make this commitment to yourself (for one month): any other time it comes to mind, say it again.

● ● ● ● ●

When you get up, say the Jesus Creed.

When you go to bed, say it again.

When you leave your house, say it again.

When you enter your house, say it one more time.

● ● ● ● ●

Why do these things? Just watch what happens to you when you begin to live the Jesus Creed. You will see how loving God and loving others begins to seep into everything you say, you do, and you think. You will also find yourself living the Jesus Creed. This is precisely why God told the Israelites to repeat the *Shema* all the time: repetition has a way of working itself into the soul and heart.

One of my students told me this story. She was nannying for a wealthy family and she didn't particularly like the kids. But it was good money and she was trying her best to like the kids (and she admitted they could be difficult). One day, on her way to that home, she came to an intersection, and as she waited for another car, the Jesus Creed came into her mind. So she said it. It calmed her, and she said this: "I was SO, SO different for a few hours and then I got cranky." The next day, she told me, she did the same thing with the same result. But she wasn't happy that she got so cranky with the kids after a couple hours. So, she said when she noticed her own irritation the next day, she stopped and said the Jesus Creed calmly one more time. She then said this to me: "Saying the Jesus Creed made SO much difference. So I started saying it more often, and you know what, Scot? I got to where I really began to love those kids. Now it's fall and I'm back in classes and I miss them."

●   ●   ●   ●   ●

Recite the Jesus Creed

happiness is a GPS
(global positional system)

●　●　●　●　●

Recite the Jesus Creed

Do you want to be happy? Do you want to feel good about yourself? Do you want to be personally satisfied and contented and tranquil and enjoy life?

Recently I did an informal survey of my Facebook "friends," wandering through their "Info" pages one by one for a long, long time. I wanted to know what my friends wanted out of life. I didn't write them and ask them, but just trusted their words on their Info pages would give me some clues. What do you think was the number-one idea that rose to the top of what they wanted from life? To enjoy life or to be personally happy.

No question about it.

Happiness is what people want out of life.

Some of my friends equate happiness with self-discovery; others think they'll find happiness by discovering love; yet others believe they'll be happy if they can challenge injustices and overcome obstacles and triumph and succeed; others want to get a good job and make good money and find a good husband or wife and have good kids in a good community; and others seem to contend that happiness comes from traveling around the world. I'm guessing that my friends are not too different from yours; every one of us is unique, but we all agree on happiness.

● ● ● ● ●

What is happiness?

● ● ● ● ●

As I read those Info pages on Facebook, though, something dawned on me. Nearly every one of my friends connected happiness with *getting something they wanted—whether what they wanted was love, friends, good jobs, experiences, travel, or even world peace.*

But what if you don't get what you want? When I was in junior high and high school, what I wanted was a successful athletic career—and it didn't matter to me whether I played in the NBA or the NFL or won a medal in track and field at the Olympics. I just wanted to rise to the top. But then one day during basketball practice in my senior year in high school something began to pop in my knee, and two weeks later I was hobbling on crutches and my athletic career was all but over. This was before the days of arthroscopy, so they cut my knee open, severing muscles and nerves and . . . well . . . the winding scar ended *what I wanted.* I had been living for a dream, and that dream, so I believed, would bring me happiness.

The dream ended. If happiness can be found only in getting what we most dream for, then happiness is almost impossible, because very few people get what they most want out of life.

Happiness eludes its devotees

We are a culture obsessed with happiness, and yet it seems to elude us. More people are depressed than perhaps at any other time in history. One recent study suggests that fifteen percent of the population of most developed countries suffers from severe depression. What do we make of this? A study from the late 1980s found that with the baby boom generation in the U.S. (those born between 1946 and 1964), depression increased tenfold, compared with the previous generations.[2] The cause? The researcher concluded that these baby boomers abandoned the example of previous generations of living for something greater than themselves and instead sought to live only for their own happiness. How ironic that the primary goal of these people's lives was the very thing that eluded them. So how do we apply this study to our purposes?

Don't seek happiness. Seek God. Seek to live according to the Jesus Creed, loving God and others, and what you'll find is that you get the happiness thrown in. In Jesus' words (Matthew 6:33): Seek first the kingdom of God and his righteousness and all these things will be given to you as well. Happiness is not something we seek; happiness comes to those who seek what is right and good and loving.

Jesus had a GPS

Like giving answers to a time-shortened pop quiz, Jesus must have been asked, "Who do you think is happy?" and he answered by listing the sort of people who are happy. We call his answers the Beatitudes.

His answers shocked his audience, and they were designed to shock them. We see the word *blessed* over and over in the Beatitudes, and I think the quest for happiness in our culture is actually the quest to be blessed.

So, who's happy according to Jesus?

The poor in spirit.
Those who are mourning someone's death.
The meek and humble.
Those whose souls ache to do what is right.
Those who see others in need and respond in mercy.
Those whose inner hearts are pure.
And those who get between fighters to bring the balm of peace.

That's seven surprises, but the next two are even more surprising:

Those who are physically persecuted and socially excluded.
And those who are verbally insulted and unjustly accused.

● ● ● ● ●

Would Jesus' list of "blessed" people be
your list?

● ● ● ● ●

It's much easier to see why peacemakers are blessed by Jesus than it is
to see how someone can be called "blessed!" for being opposed, excluded,
or accused because they follow Jesus—and some of his closest followers were crucified and martyred for following Jesus. Why call someone
blessed who suffered martyrdom? It sure looks like Jesus' idea of *blessed*
contrasts with our view of happiness. What could Jesus mean by this word
blessed?

So I sat down with my Bible open and read Matthew 5:1–16 closely,
pondering over words and sentences and connections. What jumped out at
me is that these people were blessed *because they don't fit the stereotype
of what makes a person happy*. Reading the Bible closely means consider-
ing all the angles, so I turned to the Gospel of Luke because he records
a slightly different version of Jesus' "Nine Blessed People." There Jesus
lists only Four Blessed People:

The poor
The hungry
The weeping
And the persecuted.

But I noticed something else: Jesus goes on to *denounce another group of people*. Who does he denounce?

> The rich
> The eat-everything-you-can-stuff-into-your-maw crowd
> The laughing
> And the popular.

So I pondered some more. What is the difference, or what are the differences, between the "blessed" and the "not blessed" groups? What we find guides us right to the heart of how people can be flourishingly happy and not get what they want. It starts with which word is best.

● ● ● ● ●

How are you doing on reciting the
Jesus Creed daily?

● ● ● ● ● ● ●

The word *blessed* is far richer, far deeper, and far more transcendent than the term *happy*. That word *happy*, unfortunately, makes me think of emoticons and people with big smiles and the pumped and the thrilled. I teach at North Park University. As I write this, we are grieving at North Park. Two of our students died within one week of one another. College students aren't supposed to die. Others in our community also died. One group in Jesus' list was the grieving. Jesus blessed the grieving, but he didn't mean to say, "So, someone died. Be happy!"

The president at North Park, David Parkyn, wrote all of us a note, and here are some of his words:

In years to come when we tell the story of this year at North Park death will be an important part of our story. We will tell of Jessica and Kat, two undergraduates at North Park who died within a week of each other in the spring semester. We will tell of Vernard, a seminary student, Betty, a campus administrator, and Wendy, a faculty member, who each died during the fall semester.

But today we are grieving. Our story this year doesn't ring true. We struggle to make sense of it. We have lost five beloved members of our campus community. These have been our friends and colleagues, roommates and lab partners, companions in the joy of life at North Park. We grieve this loss; we wonder why God allows such grief and loss, pain and tears in our lives individually and in our collective community life.

Stories that matter—like the story of this year at North Park—often complicate life. The story isn't being written as we expect or want. Yet in the unexpected we may discover the truth expressed in an old Spanish saying: *"Dios escribe derecho con líneas torcidas."*—God writes straight with crooked lines.—Death is part of this year's story at North Park, a story written by God with crooked lines.

But Jesus blessed the grieving (like our whole campus). Jesus blessed those who are living in the crooked lines. Why?

Because to be blessed is not getting something we want, but being the kind of person God wants us to be. Being blessed is being a person who loves God and loves others, as the Jesus Creed teaches. Sensitive, caring, loving people grieve when someone dies, and they work for peace when fights break out, and they ache to do what is right in each circumstance in life. Jesus blesses people for *being approved and loved and affirmed by God.* So, being happy according to Jesus is not at all about getting what you want or what I want. Instead, being happy *is being the person God wants you to be*. Correct that: being the person God wants you to be makes you *blessed*.

Our point: It is better to be blessed than happy. Blessed carries us through bad days; happy is only on the good days. Blessed is about loving God and loving others; happy is about loving myself (and whatever makes me happy).

● ● ● ● ●

> Being blessed is not getting something we want, but being the kind of person God wants us to be.

● ● ● ● ●

This deep and inner conviction—happiness is about what God wants and not what we want—gave Jesus a GPS to guide his followers. The poor and the persecuted, the grieving and the peacemaking, and the humble and the poor are given a GPS to navigate life. When things don't go our way, when we don't get what we want, when life's path takes a sharp curve and throws us down into the valley, when the line from where you are to where you want to go gets crooked, happiness—correct that—being *blessed* guides us through the night and into the light. Jesus' words are the GPS for his followers. They point the way when life doesn't turn out the way we hoped. Instead of equating our happiness with getting what we want, we can become happy by becoming and being the people God wants.

That's the difference between happy and blessed.

One more thing to say: the word *blessed* describes the person whose central principles are "love God" and "love others." The word *happy* describes the person whose central principle is "love myself."

● ● ● ● ●

Recite the Jesus Creed

the more Jesus expects

● ● ● ● ●

Recite the Jesus Creed

Jesus expects more from his followers.

Have you ever noticed that there are lots of folks who come to church weekly, who attend Sunday school classes, who lead Bible studies, and who "name the name," but who—and let's be honest—aren't any different morally from a Buddhist you know or an atheist friend or your teacher who doesn't even go to church? Have you ever wondered *what difference it makes (morally) to be a follower of Jesus?* Or does it even make a difference?

Some people, when they start reading passages like the Sermon on the Mount, the greatest moral discourse in history, say this sort of thing: "The big thing is to have your sins forgiven. God wants us to be obedient, but whether we are or not does not change our eternal status. Once God forgives, we're forgiven. That means we're going to heaven, obedient or not." Well, yes, God does forgive and I'm so grateful for God's gracious forgiveness.

But . . . but . . . but . . . here's the big point: forgiven followers emerge from forgiveness to follow Jesus. Genuine forgiveness creates followers of Jesus. Those who don't follow are either not forgiven or—which is another way of saying the same thing—are not followers. Followers follow, that's the bottom line. If you love God, you follow Jesus. There are no other real options. Yes, to be sure, no one follows Jesus perfectly. But begging off following Jesus because you can't be perfect is like saying you're not a student unless you get all A's. Even if your dad or some hard-nosed teacher makes you feel this way at times, it's not true. Students study, and if you're not studying at all you're not a student (even if your teachers pass you!). As students are noted by studying, so followers of Jesus are noted by following. So, once again, our question: Does it make a difference to follow Jesus?

●　●　●　●　●

Followers of Jesus follow Jesus.
That's the bottom line.

●　●　●　●　●

For Jesus it did and it still does. He expected his followers to be morally better than the major groups in his world: more spiritual than the average Pharisee, more compassionate than the politically savvy Sadducees, and more peaceful than the knife-happy Zealots. If a journalist from Rome wandered into the neighborhood of some of his followers, say they were named Schmuley and Sarah, Jesus would have expected the journalist to be able to see something morally special in them. If some landowner hired one of Jesus' followers, Jesus expected the landowner might tell him after some evening dinner that he was impressed with how Reuben or Rebekah were conducting themselves as they worked.

Jesus expected more of his followers.

Stunning words of Jesus

You might want to open your Bible to Matthew 5:17–20 to read just how Jesus told his disciples he expected *more* from them. Evidently some leaders thought Jesus was calling into question Jesus' full commitment to the "Torah" (the Law of Moses), so Jesus countered that rumor with: *Do not think that I have come to abolish the Law or the Prophets.* No, he didn't come to "abolish." Instead, as Jesus put it—and these were shocking words beyond what you can probably imagine: *I have not come to abolish them but to* ***fulfill*** *them.* Every ordinary Jew who heard Jesus say this had one immediate exclamatory question: "Who do you think you are!?"

Jesus tells them the Torah is permanent and then teaches that anyone who abolishes the Torah will be called "least in the kingdom," which is a very gentle way of warning them of the bad place after we die. Then he tells them that whoever does the Torah will be "great in the kingdom," which is a typical way of saying if they follow him they'll get to participate in God's grand eternity. Then Jesus rocks their world and reveals what he expects of his disciples:

> *Unless your righteousness surpasses [much more than]*
> *that of the Pharisees and the teachers of the law, you will*
> *certainly not [never ever] enter the kingdom of heaven.*
>
> Matthew 5:20

Let's use Jesus' terms here and say that he expects his followers to have more morals than the Pharisees and teachers of the law *because they are to have "surpassing righteousness."*

Stunning words become real-life words

Now, if you are tempted to ask "So what does that mean?" or "So what does that look like in concrete practices?" you would be just like those who heard Jesus the first time. How do we know this? It's relatively simple: we just need to read on. Jesus proceeds in the rest of Matthew's fifth chapter to give six concrete illustrations of *the more Jesus expects*.

● ● ● ● ●

Who do you know who best illustrates the *more* Jesus expects? How do they show this *more*?

● ● ● ● ●

#1   Murder occurs when you hate someone.
Followers of Jesus pursue reconciliation.

#2   Adultery occurs when you lust after a woman (or man). Followers of Jesus examine their hearts and not just their sexual behaviors.

#3   Divorce is not God's design, and permissiveness is wrong. Followers of Jesus are not to divorce unless, following sexual immorality, reconciliation is impossible.

#4   Oath-taking is not needed.
Followers of Jesus always tell the truth.

#5   Retaliation breeds a cycle of violence.
Followers of Jesus create cycles of grace and love to unravel the cycles of ungrace and vengeance.

#6   Hating an enemy is wrong.

Followers of Jesus love and pray for even their enemies and persecutors.

Just in case you didn't read Matthew's fifth chapter all the way to the end, you may have missed how Jesus closes off: *Be perfect, therefore, as your heavenly Father is perfect.* The word *perfect* is Jesus' perfect way of tying this all together: the perfect person is the one who follows these six teachings of Jesus. (Jesus, of course, never expected anyone to be sinlessly perfect, but he did expect more of his followers.)

I've thought long and hard about this chapter in the Sermon on the Mount, and I've come to these three conclusions about *the more Jesus expects*.

First, the *more* Jesus intends can be reduced to loving God and loving others, what I call the Jesus Creed. The Jesus Creed reveals that for Jesus the whole Torah is summed up in and can be reduced to loving God and loving others. Jesus is not letting you off the hook here, but instead is deepening all commands to *your relationship with God and your relationship to others.* You are a *more* follower when you love God and love others.

• • • • • • • • • • •

How is the Jesus Creed the *more* Jesus expects?

• • • • • • • • • • •

Second, the *more* means we are focused on our inner heart and our behavior — in that order. That is, love God first and that will lead to loving others. It is tempting to say, "I didn't take anyone's life" or "I didn't have (complete) sex" or "I wasn't to blame for the divorce" or "I didn't break my oath" or "I only punished a person to the degree the law permits" or "I detest the terrorists too, just as all Americans do." But Jesus wants to know what's going on inside you: Is your heart shaped by a desire to be reconciled, by a sex life that seeks to be pure, by a marriage that is shaped by love, by words that always tell the truth, by a desire not to take revenge but to bring grace, and by a relationship to those hostile to you that is marked by love? You are a *more* follower when your inner world and your outer world line up.

Third, the *more* means we really are living the *more* life. Jesus is as tired as you are of people who say they're Christians but who don't follow him. He's as wearied as you are by excuses. But the implication of this is not that you can sit back and point fingers at flabby Christian commitment and feel all right about yourself. No, Jesus really does expect his followers to be and to do more than the religious experts of our day. Including you. Right now. Here's an example of one of us who is thinking about what it means to do the "more."

As often as I can, I reflect on Jesus' call to "Come, follow me" in Matthew chapter 4, verses 18 through 22. It's not the only place in the Gospels where Jesus invites people to follow him. But for me it is the most remembered of all the places. Jesus' invitation to follow him is simple: lay behind you what occupies you and practice what he teaches. As you know, *simple* doesn't always mean *easy*. There is nothing easy about Jesus' invitation, but it is clear, simple, and doable.

For me, following Jesus is about trading up. It is about giving myself away to a greater cause, which is the kingdom of heaven. The kingdom of God is both within me and within a group of people or a society of other like-hearted people who choose to accept Jesus' invitation to follow him and let Jesus be the King of their lives. The Jesus Creed governs people who allow Jesus to be the King of their lives. The Jesus Creed, to love God and to love others, is the footing on which the kingdom of heaven comes to earth. The Jesus Creed, lived out, is a visual rendering of following Jesus.

● ● ● ● ●

Recite the Jesus Creed

spiritual branding

● ● ● ● ●

Recite the Jesus Creed

Image matters deeply for some people, so deeply they lose contact between who they really are and what their image is.

Another word we use for image today is *brand*. Some students cultivate a brand of who they are, making sure they look a certain way, act a certain way, and go to certain parties. Facebook gives us the opportunity (and temptation) to brand ourselves (falsely).

Clothing manufacturers and shoe companies invest g'zillions in their brand so that everything is permeated with their message. I think of 7 Jeans, UGG boots, Victoria Secret Pink, and Abercrombie and Fitch . . . would you be offended if I used the word *grunge*? Others react to such brands to form their resistant brands and they dress down, or let their pants hang way down, or all wear the same basic color and style of shoes and listen to the same music . . . maybe you are thinking of "emo." Maybe it's skinny jeans.

● ● ● ● ●

Feeling comfortable with yourself isn't an automatic gift when you become sixteen or eighteen.

● ● ● ● ●

But let's be really honest about something: Finding your identity and landing in a self-confident place and feeling comfortable with yourself are not automatic gifts when you become sixteen or eighteen. Part of the process of finding that identity—and this can be painful and wounding at times and can even cascade you into a funk for a long time—is to observe what others think of you and to observe how they respond to you. No one really escapes this although a few "seem" to. No one really does.

The basics are these: as a child your identity is shaped by your family and being with your family. In many ways their identity is your identity. When you enter into adolescence you begin what is called "individuation," and the process of individuation, or forming an individual identity in distinction from your parents, can be turbulent. The hardest part of all is learning to love yourself for the person God made you to be. The easiest temptation—and this is where image and brand factor in at the deepest level—is to think of yourself as others think of you or to create an image of what you want others to think of you. That means it is easy to form your identity on the basis of what others think instead of on what God thinks and instead of on what you know about yourself deep inside. It also means we can learn to *brand* ourselves in order to *sell ourselves* before others. But there really is a better, healthier way.

Spiritual branding

What God thinks of us is what really matters. Loving God first leads us on a path where branding is no longer necessary. Back up to something we've mentioned: we are easily tempted to think of ourselves on the basis of what others think of us, and then to manicure and adjust our images so they will think better of us. This self-branding actually gets deeper: *when others think approvingly of us, it can be intoxicating.* So intoxicating that we can learn to do even religious things and even spiritual practices *in order to gain the approval of others or to sustain the approval of others.*

We are tempted, then, not only to *brand* our image, but also to brand our spiritual image. It's dizzying, isn't it? But it is so true, so true we have to think about this more.

● ● ● ● ●

What is your biggest temptation when it comes
to branding yourself?
Talk to a close friend about this.
Why do you think we have this temptation?
How is this related to wanting to be in control?

● ● ● ● ●

Jesus knew some religious brand-ers, and he talked about them in Matthew 6, verses 1 through 18. This is a great section in the Bible. His word for them was "hypocrites." They branded themselves, and Jesus had strong words for them: *Be careful not to do your "acts of righteousness" in front of others, to be seen by them*. Following Jesus means that we are called to practice our faith with a focus on loving God first, as we learn from the Jesus Creed, even if that also means ignoring what others think.

Some of Jesus' contemporaries were branding themselves when they gave alms, or gave gifts of money or goods to help the poor: *So when you give to the needy, do not announce it with trumpets, as the hypocrites do in the synagogues and on the streets, to be honored by others*. Charity is good, Jesus would say, but charity giving in order to wave your personal brand of generosity is hypocrisy. Some of them were branding themselves when they prayed: *And when you pray, do not be like the hypocrites, for they love to pray standing in the synagogues and on the street corners to be seen by others*. Some of them were branding themselves when they fasted:

When you fast, do not look somber as the hypocrites do, for they disfigure their faces to show others they are fasting.

Yes, Jesus sketches this is in almost comic form: givers tooting horns, pray-ers praying aloud on street corners, and fasters disfiguring faces so they look miserable. Go ahead and LOL. But remember this too: these caricatures of Jesus boldly warn *us* not to brand our spiritual practices, and it is all too easy to fall into this trap.

Sure, it is easy to make fun of Jesus' opponents, but we need to think a little more about our own world. Sometimes your church leaders or pastors do these very things: in some churches, children get candy from their Sunday school teachers when they turn in their completed "God time" cards the following Sunday. Maybe your youth pastor has said he'll shave his head if a certain number of people sign up for an event. I know the heart behind each of these incentives is to get young people to take their faith more seriously or even to get students introduced to Jesus—which is a very good thing—but our motives are much more important.

So, let's think about this a little bit: You should read the Bible because it helps you and honors God, not so that "spiritual leaders" will pat you on the head. You should invite your friends to church-related events so that they can experience the joy and fullness of following Jesus, not so that your youth pastor is impressed. Maybe you need to ask yourself these questions:

> Am I doing this because I'm looking for God?
> Am I doing this for the sake of my parents?
> Am I doing this for acceptance with others?
> Am I doing this so my pastor or leader will approve of me?

Because what God thinks is the only thing that matters.

Followers focus on God

Instead of branding our spirituality, Jesus wants us to *focus on God*: when we give, we thank God for what God has given us; when we pray, we talk to God and do so in such a manner that we ignore what others think of us; when we fast—and this should only be done with the knowledge of your physician—we are to do so with our minds and hearts fixed on God. Genuine love of God, the opening part of the Jesus Creed, is about a life that is focused on God and not distracted by how much attention we get for our relationship.

● ● ● ● ●

What happens to branding when we live by the Jesus Creed?

● ● ● ● ●

I want to interrupt our thoughts for a moment to ask this question: Do you know anyone who has "been together" with another person *solely* to be known for being together with that person? Now tell the truth: What did you think of that person? ("Not much!" is the right answer.) Yet, we are tempted like the dickens to do that very thing in spiritual actions: to do something in order to gain public benefits.

There's a twist right in the middle of our passage in Matthew 6. Clearly, Jesus is teaching about the temptation to hypocrisy in branding our spirituality, and in Jesus' world that meant the world of charity, prayer, and fasting. But in the middle of this we find the Lord's Prayer, and that passage is not about impressing others but about *impressing God with our prayers*. If there's comedy in how Jesus describes the hypocrites when they give charity, pray, and fast, there's even more comedy in these lines:

*And when you pray, do not keep on babbling like pagans,
for they think they will be heard because of their many
words.*

These pray-ers thought God would listen

> if they had long-winded prayers,
> if they used fancy words, and
> if they prayed all night long.

They evidently thought they could impress God with what they knew and with the degree of their spirituality. Jesus crushed that idea with one quick jab: *Do not be like them, for your Father knows what you need before you ask him.*

Which brings us right back to the same point: *religious practices and spiritual disciplines are about God, not about what we can do to impress others or to impress God.*

● ● ● ● ●

When are you tempted to do something spiritual in order to be seen by others?

● ● ● ●

What a relief

It's a huge relief to listen to Jesus blow branding out of the water. The one safe place we can go where no one can start evaluating us, the one safe place we can enter where others cannot stare at us, and the one safe place where we don't have to worry about our brand or our image or what others think is the presence of God. In that place, God accepts us for who we are, and he invites us to engage in spiritual practices in order to love him more so we can love others more.

So let me make a suggestion to you so you can practice being in God's presence and avoid the stares of others and the judgment of others. Let me suggest that you begin giving some of your time to a charitable organization. Here are the steps:

First, ask God for wisdom on which charity you choose.

Second, tell your parents or one or two of your best friends what you are going to do, but make sure you tell them only because it is wise for them to know what you are doing. Please avoid telling them so they'll say, "My, I'm so proud of you." They may say that anyway, but you'll have to utter a quick prayer like this: "Thanks, God, for this chance to help others."

Third, commit yourself to weekly or monthly participation for, say, six months.

Fourth, do your charitable work without telling anyone.

Fifth, keep not telling anyone.

Sixth, when you get home, spend time with God thanking God for the opportunity and talking to God about what you are learning. Include in your prayer a clear idea that this act of charity does not impress God or make you any more spiritual than anyone else.

Seventh, keep the whole thing a secret between you and God.

Here's my prediction: in six months or sooner you'll see just why Jesus had to tell his followers that branding their spiritual disciplines was a dangerous road to travel. Keep it a secret. Keep on keeping it a secret.

● ● ● ● ●
Recite the Jesus Creed

the Lord's Prayer

● ● ● ● ●

Recite the Jesus Creed

I don't know how you feel about this, but I'm not a big fan of football teams huddling together before a game and, after listening to a pep talk to "walk all over them" or to "beat 'em crazy" or to "go out there and be the warrior" or "take no prisoners," then lowering the tone just enough to say a quick "Our Father who art in heaven. . . ."

I don't know if that causes inner turmoil for you as it does for me, but it sure does bug me. I wish they'd pray what they are really thinking. Like, "God, we want to whup 'em and we want you, Master Warrior, on our side! Yah!" followed by some high fives or chest bumps. What, I think to myself, does high-fiving and chest-bumping have to do with the Lord's Prayer?

Have you ever wondered why so many pray the Lord's Prayer? Here's my suspicion, and you can chat with your friends about this, and I think you might be surprised how many have opinions about it. I think many people believe this special prayer by Jesus is *magical*. Just repeating the words—and many of us can recite these words without even knowing what we are saying—seems to make people feel approved by God or in contact with God or make them feel they have done the right thing.

Newsflash: the Lord's Prayer is not magic.

● ● ● ● ●

The Lord's Prayer is not magic.
No prayer is.

● ● ● ● ●

Not every world religion shares this nonmagical view when it comes to their Holy Scriptures or their special prayers, sometimes called mantras. Followers of Islam who don't speak Arabic must learn Arabic even to read the Koran because they believe that simply reading the words of the Koran in the original language is beneficial. Not so with the Bible and not so with the way Jesus taught us about prayer. As Jesus already made clear, the mindless repetition of any prayer is not what he's after. He doesn't want us to repeat the Lord's Prayer mindlessly but to use the Lord's Prayer mindfully.

In fact, the Lord's Prayer is a special prayer for followers of Jesus.

And, no matter how some hear this, I'll say it boldly: this prayer is *only for followers of Jesus.* I want to make a second bold claim about the Lord's Prayer: *followers of Jesus need to recite this prayer every day.* Why? Because Jesus told us to. Repeating the Lord's Prayer is neither magic nor a mantra, but instead the Master's way of prayer.

The disciples' request

Do you know how we got the Lord's Prayer? The Bible tells us in Luke's eleventh chapter:[*]

> *One day Jesus was praying in a certain place. When he finished, one of his disciples said to him, "Lord, teach us to pray, just as John taught his disciples."*

---

[*] Matthew 6:9–13 has a different version, but our concern for now is not the longer version there.

He said to them,

When you pray, say:
Father,
> *hallowed be your name,*
> *your kingdom come.*
Give us each day our daily bread.
Forgive us our sins,
>> *for we also forgive everyone who sins against us.*
>> *And lead us not into temptation.*

The first followers of Jesus observed that John the Baptist was teaching his disciples to pray, and that probably means he gave them a special prayer to recite, so Jesus' followers thought they should have one. Jesus thought so too, and he gave them a prayer to recite. Some of us call it the "Lord's Prayer" while others call it the "Our Father." (Check out what it is called in the foreign language you are learning.)

I have put in bold letters some very important points that need to be observed. The word *When* means "whenever," which is another way of saying "every time you pray." And the word *say* could be translated as "recite." Put together, these words tell us Jesus taught his disciples that *every time they prayed, they should say or use this prayer.* I love to say the Lord's Prayer, and I say it often. The longer I've said the Lord's Prayer, the more meaningful it has become.

● ● ● ● ●

What do you think of reciting
the Lord's Prayer every time you pray?
What do you think "whenever you pray" means?

● ● ● ● ●

Why the Lord's Prayer?

Why? The Lord's Prayer puts into words the central vision of Jesus for his followers: observe that the themes of the Jesus Creed are present here. The Jesus Creed concentrated the entire will of God on two ideas: love God and love others. The Lord's Prayer has the same two-beat emphasis. It teaches us to love God by praying to God and to love others by praying for others. So, I want to reframe the Lord's Prayer so you can see just how this prayer expresses the Jesus Creed, and this time I'll use the words from Matthew's slightly longer version (and probably the one you memorized):

Those who love God say these things:

Our Father in heaven,
hallowed be your name,
your kingdom come,
your will be done,
on earth as it is in heaven.

Those who love others pray these things for others:

Give us today our daily bread.
And forgive us our debts,
as we also have forgiven our debtors.
And lead us not into temptation,
but deliver us from the evil one.[*]

Matthew 6:9–13

Here's the gist of the Lord's Prayer:

---

[*] Matthew's version is often quoted with some extra words, though those words were not in the original text of Matthew. Instead, they were used to close off the prayer in early Christian worship, and some scribes couldn't resist adding them in; I don't blame you if you add them too! "For yours is the kingdom and the power and the glory forever. Amen."

- Those who love God approach God as the Father who dwells in the heavens.
- Those who love God speak to and about and live before an all-holy God, and so they revere who God is and are careful about how they speak of God.
- And those who love God yearn for God's kingdom and will to be done on earth just as it is done in the very presence of God.

• • • • • • • • • • •

Discuss with a friend or your small group
or a youth group how each of the requests
in the Lord's Prayer expresses either
love for God or love for others.

• • • • • • • • • • • •

- Those who love others yearn that others will have sufficient food for the day, and in a day of scarcity this prayer was a daily necessity.
- Those who love God pray that they will be forgiving people and will create a cycle of grace.
- Those who love God pray that none of us will be thrown off course but will walk in love and holiness and beauty.
- And those who love God respect the dark forces of this world enough to ask God on a regular basis to preserve them from the evil one's assaults.

Seriously, what more do you need for guidance for your prayers?

An assignment

At the end of one of my classes called "Jesus of Nazareth," I make an offer to my students, and if you were one of my students I'd make the same offer to you. If they say the Jesus Creed (or the Lord's Prayer) at least one time for five days a week over the summer break or the Christmas break, I'll buy them lunch (for the summer assignment) or a cup of coffee (for the Christmas break assignment). (You might want to know that more come to my office and ask me to pay up after the summer than after Christmas; it appears Christmas is far more distracting than summer.)

So, here's your assignment:

- For one month,
- Every morning when you get up and every night when you go to bed,
- And any time it comes to mind between those two times,
- Say the Lord's Prayer.

I encourage you to say it aloud if possible, and to say it slowly. Those who say it quickly tend to say it to get done with it more than those who say it slowly.

• • • • • • • • •

An Assignment: For one month, in the morning, in the evening, and anytime it comes to mind, say the Lord's Prayer, along with the Jesus Creed, and say them both aloud.

• • • • • • • • • •

But the catch on this one is just like the Jesus Creed: the more often you say the Lord's Prayer, the more often you see just how powerful this prayer is. As one who has been saying the Lord's Prayer several times a day (and sometimes more than several) for years, I can witness to this: the Lord's Prayer expresses the core of Jesus' vision, and its lines emerge into my mind constantly. If you want to know what it means to follow Jesus, listen to the Lord's Prayer and the Jesus Creed.

> The Lord's Prayer is not just a prayer for me.
> It's my guide.
> It's the Jesus Creed in the form of prayer.

The Lord's Prayer is inspiring. It is also challenging. When I pray the Lord's Prayer I am moved to be a more deeply committed follower. Followers of Jesus trade up or give away themselves to a greater cause. The Lord's Prayer represents that greater cause. My family and I pray the Lord's Prayer each day before we eat our dinner together. We do this in order that we might be reminded of four things: 1) who God is, 2) who we are, 3) our relationships with others, and 4) our roles in caring for this world.

What do we learn when we let the Lord's Prayer shape us and form us and mold us?

Who God is:

> God is Holy
> God is Ruler of all
> God is Provider

Who we are:

>   We are sinners who need God

Our relationships with others:

>   We are to be about reconciliation or about peace

Our roles in caring for this world:

>   Earth is God's and we are its caretakers

If I forget to lead my family in the Lord's Prayer before our meal together, someone quickly reminds me. We do this at mealtime because it is usually the only time we are all together for a period of time. For us, it isn't a rote behavior but rather a living expression. The Lord's Prayer is our connection back to the Jesus Creed every day.

We begin at this point something new. In the chapters up to this point we have both begun and ended each chapter with the Jesus Creed. From this point on we will begin the chapter with the Jesus Creed but end it by reciting the Lord's Prayer. Notice what happens to you as you let these two wonderful teachings of Jesus begin to shape your life more and more.

●　●　●　●　●

Say the Lord's Prayer

CHAPTER 6
forgiveness

● ● ● ● ●

Recite the Jesus Creed

The best thing I've ever heard about forgiveness is worth repeating every time I think about forgiveness. The great British author C. S. Lewis, just after World War II and when the British were still digging out from the rubble created by Hitler's *Blitzkrieg* bombings, on a radio talk said this: "Every one says forgiveness is a lovely idea, until they have something to forgive." Some met C. S. Lewis's words with howls of derision and mocking. So Lewis pushed back: "I am not trying to tell you . . . what I could do. . . . I am telling you what Christianity is. I did not invent it. And there, right in the middle of it, I find 'Forgive us our sins as we forgive those that sin against us.'"

● ● ● ● ●

C. S. Lewis: "Every one says forgiveness is a lovely idea, until they have something to forgive." Ponder this wisdom.

● ● ● ● ●

"It is made perfectly clear that if we do not forgive we shall not be forgiven. There are not two ways about it. What are we to do?"[3] So Lewis continues. Are you ready for those words? Maybe you're thinking it's a little (or very) bold of Jesus to connect our being forgiven with our forgiving of others. Bold or not, Jesus said it.

I could try to explain away Jesus' demanding words about forgiveness, but Jesus doesn't want us to. He said this because he meant it, and he put it in neon lights when he made it one of the lines of the Lord's Prayer—and that means we will have to hear it or say it every day (for at least a month).

Just in case you think this is an exceptional statement by Jesus, and a kind of one-off crazy idea, I want to remind you that he said things like this often enough to make us think he really meant business with this idea of being forgiving people. Here's why: someone who genuinely loves others forgives. Why? Because God is loving and God is forgiving and God forgives us. God is the model of how to live. That means if we are to love others as we love ourselves it means we will forgive them because we'd want to be forgiven too.

Jesus Creed students love others, and loving others means we learn to forgive others. Let me bring us back to reality with C. S. Lewis one more time: forgiveness is a great idea . . . until the person you are to forgive is someone you don't even like or someone who said something that really hurt.

Jesus came to transform us, not just comfort us.

Jesus' words

> Therefore, if you are offering your gift at the altar and there remember that your brother or sister has something against you, leave your gift there in front of the altar. First go and be reconciled to that person; then come and offer your gift.
>
> Matthew 5:23–24

> For if you forgive others when they sin against you, your heavenly Father will also forgive you. But if you do not forgive others their sins, your Father will not forgive your sins.
>
> Matthew 6:14–15

Then Peter came to Jesus and asked, "Lord, how many
times shall I forgive someone who sins against me? Up to
seven times?" Jesus answered, "I tell you, not seven times,
but seventy-seven times."   Matthew 18:21–22

Father, forgive them, for they do not know what they are
doing.   Luke 23:34

Let's get this straight. These are the words of Jesus. Four very clear times
he pushed toward forgiving others. He knew exactly what he was saying.

The operative principle of first-century Jewish and Roman society, and
ours is no different, is called the *lex talionis*, the principle that a crime's
punishment is to meet the crime. No more and no less. But in the face of
the *lex talionis* Jesus thought the desire for vengeance or vindication was
not the way of God. Instead, he practiced the Jesus Creed of loving God
and loving others. Love for Jesus meant the long-term goal was to offer
forgiveness, to forgive, and to reconcile—even with enemies and those
who have committed offenses against us. You can't love someone and hate
that same person at the same time.

● ● ● ● ●

You can't love someone and hate that
same person at the same time.

● ● ● ● ●

Now, before we get too crazy on this and drop all sense of morality and
even decency, we need to make some observations. Forgiveness is serious
business, and we need to get our heads around it before we begin doing
foolish things.

How to live this?

First, Jesus' teaching about forgiving others is the kingdom vision. It will not always happen, and in some cases it can't happen (when a person dies before reconciliation) and in other cases it shouldn't until serious issues are addressed (like abuse and violence). But, the kingdom vision is a vision of followers of Jesus living together in a reconciled state. The following parable of Jesus reveals the kingdom vision; it's a bit long, but it's a very good story that shows what Jesus means, and so I want you to take the time to read it carefully:

> *Therefore, the kingdom of heaven is like a king who wanted to settle accounts with his servants. As he began the settlement, a man who owed him ten thousand bags of gold was brought to him. Since he was not able to pay, the master ordered that he and his wife and his children and all that he had be sold to repay the debt.*

> *The servant fell on his knees before him. "Be patient with me," he begged, "and I will pay back everything." The servant's master took pity on him, canceled the debt and let him go.*

> *But when that servant went out, he found one of his fellow servants who owed him a hundred silver coins. He grabbed him and began to choke him. "Pay back what you owe me!" he demanded.*

> *His fellow servant fell to his knees and begged him, "Be patient with me, and I will pay you back."*

> *But he refused. Instead, he went off and had the man thrown into prison until he could pay the debt. When the other servants saw what had happened, they were greatly*

distressed and went and told their master everything that had happened.

Then the master called the servant in. "You wicked servant," he said, "I canceled all that debt of yours because you begged me to. Shouldn't you have had mercy on your fellow servant just as I had on you?" In anger his master handed him over to the jailers to be tortured, until he should pay back all he owed.

This is how my heavenly Father will treat each of you unless you forgive a brother or sister from your heart.

Matthew 18:23–35

What's the download (or upload) from this parable? In one crisp sentence: forgiveness isn't an option for Jesus' followers. It's how they live. This parable affirms in graphic realities that forgiveness marks, shapes, forms, and guides the follower of Jesus.

Now a few more observations about the inner workings of forgiveness, and each of these can be so significant that you may want to sit down with friends to discuss them or find a place alone just to ponder each:

- Forgiveness is something God does or a condition that God shows us—and there's no better place to see this than when Jesus, at the cross, forgave those who were putting him to death. God forgives on the basis of Jesus' death, and any forgiveness we offer—if we are followers of Jesus—needs to begin with God's forgiveness. God creates the cycle of grace, and our forgiveness is tapping into that mercy-flow of God. We don't forgive first; God does. So, what Jesus is saying is that forgiven people, if they are really forgiven, become grace-giving, forgiving people. If they are not grace-giving people, there's something seriously wrong.

● ● ● ● ●

Forgiven people become grace-giving, forgiving people.

● ● ● ● ●

- When the cycle is one of justice upon justice or justice as nothing more than vindication or even justice without forgiveness, the world in which we live continues to repeat and escalate the cycle of violence. Jesus wanted to break the cycle of vindication and violence by offering forgiveness and pursuing reconciliation— and we get to participate in this grace cycle by preemptive strikes of forgiveness when we have the chance.

- Forgiveness does not suppress or cover up the wrong action of someone else. Forgiveness does not ignore or pretend something wasn't as bad as it really was. If someone has lied about you or wrongfully harmed you or abused you, that wrongful act must be acknowledged before forgiveness can be granted. Forgiveness begins with justice, but it does not stop at justice.

- Repentance is often needed before reconciliation can occur. You, as the wronged person, might personally, emotionally, psychologically, and spiritually forgive someone and release yourself from being the victim of a wrong action, but until the injuring person repents from what they have done, you can't be genuinely reconciled. Sometimes this may not happen ever. It often takes two to complete the fullness of the forgiveness cycle.

There is some good, good news here: forgiveness can be a magical display of God's grace. When it's done right, the watching world will be amazed. Forgiving someone who has wronged you is one of those "I can't believe anyone would do that" kinds of acts. Forgiveness displays the Jesus Creed kind of life.

In 2006, a gunman entered a one-room Amish school building in Pennsylvania and shot ten schoolchildren, killing five of them before turning the gun on himself. Any person in his right mind would immediately jump to anger, vengeance, rage, and "justice as vindication," but this community of Amish Christ-followers handled itself quite differently. Within hours after the shootings, the Amish community reached out to the family of the gunman and extended forgiveness to them. Some of them attended the funeral of the gunman, and the gunman's widow was invited to one of the children's funerals. In an open letter to the Amish community, the widow said this: "Your love for our family has helped to provide the healing we so desperately need. . . . Your compassion has reached beyond our family, beyond our community, and is changing our world. . . ."

Forgiveness is a shocking, audacious act. It's not easy, but it's powerful and it brings healing.

We need to back up so we can move this idea forward: you, at the personal level, can be held captive to what someone has done to you, and you can choose, by not pursuing forgiveness, to let that person's behavior identify you and haunt you. Or, you can choose not to let that person's evil deed or wrongful act define you, by releasing yourself from what that person did. I believe at times you simply have to choose to let go of what someone did to you and to live in the grace of God, even if that person never acknowledges what he or she has done.

The lovely idea now becomes real

Each of us has someone to forgive. This Jesus Creed life seems so cool and so hopeful and so warm and lovely, until we realize that the one we are called to love by extending forgiveness is someone we don't like or, worse yet, someone we have come to despise and perhaps even hate.

Jesus knows exactly what the Jesus Creed means when it comes to forgiveness. People made fun of him because of the rumors that circulated that he was an illegitimate child. People tried to harm him and chase him down. His own brothers (and probably sisters) didn't believe him at first. Some of those who followed him eventually gave up on him and walked away. One of his closest followers betrayed him to the authorities and he was put to death on a cross.

Stop right here and listen to this: From that very (unjust) cross Jesus said, "Father, forgive them."

● ● ● ● ●

Jesus knows exactly what the Jesus Creed means when it comes to forgiveness. Do we? Do you?

● ● ● ● ●

The best part of this, if there is a "best," is that God has forgiven us of our sins — our own lies and our own sinful thoughts and our sinful behaviors — and God invites you and me to tap into his ocean of grace to drink in God's own power to forgive.

Followers of Jesus live the Jesus Creed kind of life, and that means that we love others enough to pursue forgiveness and reconciliation. It takes two to complete the cycle, but you are called to be the one with the hand of forgiveness in the open position.

Be careful but be courageous.

● ● ● ● ●

Say the Lord's Prayer

CHAPTER 7
what are your top four?

● ● ● ● ●
Recite the Jesus Creed

When you think about your community and your friends and your school, what do you think is prized the most? What are the top four most important things to have or acquire? Look around and think awhile about this. Here's another way of asking the same question: What would you say are the top four desired items for people at your school? (Like popularity or success or looks.) The space below can be used to write out what you think your school values the most. In the right-hand column write out your top four desired items, and be as honest as you can be. (Don't cheat and look ahead.)

The Top Four Desired Items.

People at your school	You
#1	
#2	
#3	
#4	

Now give a good look at each list one more time and ask this: Did you include the W-word for either list? At the top of the world in which Jesus lived, and at the top of Jesus' own list would be the word *wisdom*. Did you think of it? (I'm guessing not. There's a reason this term has fallen out of favor, and it's not good. I hope this chapter can get the W-word back on the list.)

Jesus was **wise**, and Jesus lived in a world that valued **wisdom**, the W-word, in its top four desired items. Elderly gray-headed or bald men and elderly gray-headed women were a treasured resource in those days. Jesus' world valued wisdom above getting married, above getting a good job, above money, above fame, above celebrity, above success, above prestige, above education at the right schools, above achievements in sports, and above what anyone looked like. Jesus' world valued wisdom over youth. One of the finest compliments showered on a deceased woman or man was "She was wise" or "He was wise."

But what is wisdom? *Wisdom is living in God's world in God's way.* Jesus was wise, and at times wise ideas just flowed from his lips. Because God is love, a wise life is the Jesus Creed life. To love God and to love others as ourselves is wisdom. These two commitments to love guide all of Jesus' wisdom.

● ● ● ● ● ● ● ● ●

Jesus' world valued wisdom over youth.

What would such a commitment

look like today?

● ● ● ● ● ● ● ● ●

Four aspects of wisdom

At the beginning of Matthew's seventh chapter appear four apparently random ideas. But this was how wisdom was often taught: crisp, clear, and often unrelated bits of wisdom were connected to one another. Here are the four pieces of wisdom seen in Matthew 7:

> *judging others,*
> *holding sacred things sacred,*
> *praying to God as the good God,*
> *and finding a moral compass for all of life.*

Let's look at each one of these and see why Jesus put wisdom in his top four desired items. In what follows I want to look at four teachings of Jesus that illustrate his focus on wisdom—these four are not Jesus' top four items, but they are illustrations of wisdom, which is at the top of Jesus' list.

#1 *Judging others*

Here are the words of Jesus: *Do not judge, or you too will be judged. For in the same way you judge others, you will be judged, and with the measure you use, it will be measured to you.* Jesus loves human beings, and therefore he prohibits his followers from judging other human beings—which means taking the place of God and condemning fellow human beings. You can't love God and love others and spend your time hating and judging others. You have to choose a kingdom love-style of life. But this love-style doesn't mean blanket tolerance of everything everyone does. Jesus surely wasn't a blanket-tolerance kind of person.

All you have to do is sit down and read one Gospel from beginning to end and you will see that Jesus utters one moral judgment after another. In the sixth chapter of Matthew he calls some people "hypocrites." So, whatever Jesus means, he doesn't mean we are called to be morally spineless or absolutely tolerant of the behaviors of others. Murder is wrong, and it's wrong to say it's right and it's also wrong not to say it's wrong. Now here's what's so important: *agreeing with Jesus that something is wrong is not the kind of judgmentalism that Jesus speaks of here.* Instead, he's talking about humans assuming they are God and appointed to stand up and tell everyone who is right and who is wrong and who will go to hell and who won't.

●　●　●　●　●

Ponder how we have to be morally discerning and not morally condemning.

●　●　●　●　●

Here's where the wisdom of Jesus is so clear. Jesus gives two *reasons* we need to avoid assuming the judgment seat. First, it's always easier to see someone else's faults than our own, and Jesus tells his followers that the measuring stick they use on others will be used on themselves. The second reason is that we've all got faults, and ours just might be bigger than theirs! Jesus tells this comically: why not first remove the big ol' plank poking out of your eyelid before picking on the particle of dust in your friend's eye!

Wise followers of Jesus follow Jesus in not being The Judge.

Wise followers of Jesus love others and therefore can't be The Judge.

Here is a perfect way of saying what Jesus taught: we either have eyes of compassion for others or we develop eyes of comparison.

Eyes of compassion vs. eyes of comparison

I struggle mightily with this, yet I know not judging others is fundamental to my life as a follower of Jesus. But . . . it's not easy.

A few weeks ago I stood in line at a department store in the suburbs next to a man who smelled funny and who was wearing clothes that looked as though he had gotten them out of the trash. They were definitely clothes that someone else had clearly thrown away. I thought the man was homeless and thought to myself, "How did he get all the way down here?" (I live about thirty miles outside the city limits.) He was standing in line to buy socks, T-shirts and underwear. I was buying markers and coloring books for my kids.

The line was long and there was a problem with the register so it was taking forever. My kids were restless because we were on our way to camp for the weekend. One of my sons was teasing the other, and in doing so he accidently bumped into the man who smelled funny and who was wearing someone else's old clothes. I said to my sons, "Boys! Knock it off!" The smelly man looked at me and said, "That's okay. Boys will be boys," and he smiled at me. When he smiled at me I noticed that his teeth were bright white. Quickly (in my head, of course), I thought, this doesn't match up. His clothes are someone else's throwaway clothes and he smells like he hasn't showered in weeks and yet his teeth are perfect. "What is with that?" I asked myself.

When the man got to the register the women working the register noticed him. She called him by his name and said, "How is the clean-up going?" He responded by saying, "Okay. Long hours, and this heat is wearing me down." I came to find out this man wasn't the poor, out-of-place homeless urban dweller I thought he was. He was a suburbanite just like me who smelled funny and was wearing throwaway clothes because earlier that week his house had a fire and nearly burned to the ground.

My eyes of comparison had fooled me again! Had I been looking through my eyes of compassion I might have had more time to think about ways I might have been able to brighten his day. I should have bought his items. Instead, my eyes of comparison led me to questions in my head I was so anxious to figure out that I couldn't even see a fellow human being in need standing right in front of me.

Oh, God, that we all might have our eyes of comparison blinded so that we might see more clearly through our eyes of compassion.

The wise way is to look through eyes of compassion.

#2   *Holding sacred things sacred*

One way the Jews taught wisdom was to give a graphic moral image instead of telling people exactly what to do. Jesus does just this with this beautifully wise statement: Do not give dogs what is sacred; do not throw your pearls to pigs. No one knows exactly what "what is sacred" means and no one knows exactly what "pearls" means, but everyone who hears this knows what Jesus is getting at: we need to hold sacred things sacred, and we need to avoid holding sacred things up for contempt.

Here's an example of living this wisdom of Jesus: there's a time to talk about Jesus and a time not to talk about Jesus. If you are hanging with your friends after a sporting event, and everyone is laughing and having a great time, and the typical conversation involves ripping on others or trash-talking someone, that it is not the time to say, "Anyone want to talk about Jesus?" What is most likely to happen is that someone will then rip on Jesus. Loving God and loving others means learning to talk about sacred things at the right time.

When you've got someone's ear on a walk or when you're in a heart-to-heart talk, the sacred can be treated sacredly. Wisdom is to know the difference and to act wisely.

Wise followers of Jesus follow Jesus in holding sacred things sacred.

#3   *Praying to God as the good God*

Every follower of Jesus at times wonders about his or her faith. You do and I do. At times it's not much more than a fleeting thought—Why did God permit the earthquake in Haiti?—and it goes away. Other times it begins to haunt us, and the "Why did God permit the earthquake?"

question leads us to probe deeper and deeper into Jesus' teachings and into his wisdom.

I want you to know the truth about doubts. You don't need to fear your doubts or suppress them. We cannot discuss this at length, but we can observe that once a person encounters a potent doubt and they wrestle it for a while, that person's faith learns to carry that doubt within their faith. It doesn't so much go away as it gets carried. An encounter with a hard doubt rarely disappears; instead, our faith learns to expand so we carry on in our faith *with our doubt*.

Wisdom knows how to live with doubt.

● ● ● ● ●

How does doubt become part of our faith journey?

● ● ● ● ●

I believe this is why Jesus said what he did in Matthew 7:7–11, and here are a few of the more important lines: *Ask and it will be given to you; seek and you will find; knock and the door will be opened to you.* And *If you, then, though you are evil, know how to give good gifts to your children, how much more will your Father in heaven give good gifts to those who ask him!*

The issue here is that some of Jesus' followers are concerned whether or not God will give them good things. Perhaps they were wondering if God would provide food and supplies in their future missionary work (read about that in Matthew 10). Perhaps they were wondering if God would keep them safe. And Jesus perceived the real issue is that they didn't believe God really was good. So, Jesus' whole point in these verses is to connect his followers to God, to connect his followers to the God who is altogether good, and then to connect them to the answers to their prayers as being good as well. God is good; everything that comes from God is good. Wisdom trusts.

Wise followers of Jesus follow Jesus in trusting that God is altogether good—even when they are struggling with doubt.

#4   *A moral compass for all of life*

It was hard to gather all the commandments of the Old Testament—and there are, if you remember from the first chapter, 613 of them—and find a handle that put them into simple clarity so one could live obediently before God all day long. Jesus gathered them all together in two ways. He tells his followers that the whole Torah can be reduced brilliantly to loving God and loving others. That is the Jesus Creed.

The second way is our fourth illustration of wisdom, and it's nearly the same as the Jesus Creed. Jesus gives us the Golden Rule: *So in everything, do to others what you would have them do to you, for this sums up the Law and the Prophets* (Matthew 7:12).

Here's a simple bit of wisdom that, if you try to live by it day in and day out, will challenge your moral life down to the deepest fibers. Try to do to others—beginning at home with your siblings and your mom and dad, and then with your friends, and then with your teachers—only what you would want them to do to you. And reverse it: try not to do to them what you would never want done to you.

Like the Jesus Creed, where Jesus tells us to love others *as we love ourselves*, so is also the Golden Rule: do to others *what you would have them do to you*. This is not selfish. Instead, it's a profound grasp of human nature: the moment we begin to think about others the way we think about ourselves, we become profoundly wise (and loving) persons.

Wise followers follow Jesus in finding the Golden Rule as a moral compass for life.

Among the top four desired items for Jesus would have been the W-word: wisdom. Here are four wise teachings of Jesus. If we love God and Jesus, if we love others, we will follow these four wise teachings of Jesus. They will guide us into the wise life of loving God and loving others.

It takes a lifetime to become wise. Your lifetime begins right now.

Go for the W-word!

●   ●   ●   ●   ●

Say the Lord's Prayer

focused following

• • • • •

Recite the Jesus Creed

Jesus was big on money, or maybe it would be more accurate to say he was so big on money because he was very little on money and possessions and things. He was little on money because he was big on loving God and loving others. And if you are big on loving God and big on loving others, you can't at the same time be big on money and possessions. You have to choose which will be the big thing for you.

• • • • •

Jesus was very big on little money.

• • • • •

If Jesus were to show up in the USA tomorrow and wander through the homes and closets and cars and wallets and purses of those who claim to be his followers, he'd weep. Of that I'm sure. I know that's an act of imagination on my part, but what he says about money and possessions can shock the Westerner but good.

It's wintertime in the Chicago area. Between writing the paragraph you just read and this one I opened up the laundry and pulled some clothes out, and on my way upstairs I grabbed my nice coffee mug from my desk that is surrounded by lots of books, some of them quite expensive, and then I walked upstairs in my warm home and washed the mug in a nice sink next to my espresso coffee machine, and then I sorted out the clothes and put them away in nice wooden drawers. Then I put on a warm jacket and chose a warm stocking cap and put on some Columbia gloves, and I took off my lined Crocs and put on my Rainbow leather boots, and then I opened my garage door with a garage door opener. Then I moved my big ol' snow blower into the opening of the garage and blew snow for fifteen minutes, some of it happily landing in my neighbor's territory, and then I came back inside, drank a glass of filtered water, and turned on my espresso maker for another cup of latte, and while drinking my latte I watched a few minutes of news on a flat-screen TV that is mounted to the wall in a four-season room . . . and then I turned it off with a remote control and returned to my desk. Did I do anything special here? No, in fact, I didn't. This is the new normal for suburbanites. Nothing special here. Our home is small if measured against many in our community. What's more, many are paying five times as much in taxes, and our clothing is nothing special and our cars are nothing special and . . . and . . . and. Enough about my ordinary life and the rationalizations we use to say we're really not rich (but others are).

Take a stroll through the American dream with the kingdom dream

Take a stroll through your day, or just one hour in your day, and jot down the possessions and things that are available to you. *We assume these things are normal and we assume what we own is ours, and any idea to the contrary quickly flits across our screen (if we are even noticing).* What I'm describing is the American dream. When it comes to the American dream, Jesus is not an American. His heart is into the kingdom dream, and he challenges each of us to reconsider our part in the American dream by living for the kingdom dream.

● ● ● ● ●

> Take a stroll through your day
> and observe what is your "normal" when
> it comes to possessions and needs and wants.

● ● ● ● ●

No one has challenged this notion of living for the American dream more than a friend of ours named Shane Claiborne. Shane was just a regular teenage Christian who described himself as someone who would get born again and *again* every summer at camp. He thought there had to be more to life than just living the so-called Christian life and then going to heaven when you die. In college, his professors began to challenge his long-held notion of what the Christian life is truly about. After spending time with Mother Teresa in Calcutta, he came back to the States and began to devote his time and energies on behalf of the poor and forgotten. He now lives in a poverty-stricken community in urban Philadelphia, takes no income, and speaks all over the world on these issues. We recommend you read one of his books, but do so at your own peril: he's bound to challenge you deeply.[4]

American dream vs. kingdom dream. I wonder what Jesus would think of a heart-focused commitment to the great American dream of financial security and owning more than enough of everything and having a nice house on a nice street with nice kids who have nice friends and who go to nice schools and who will recycle the same nice American dream their parents had. Read these words from Jesus and ponder what he says in light of how you live, and see that what he wants you to do is to focus all of your love and all of your life on God.

For where your treasure is, there your heart will be also.
                                                    Matthew 6:21

You cannot serve both God and money.

Matthew 6:24

Therefore I tell you, do not worry about your life, what you will eat or drink; or about your body, what you will wear. Is not life more important than food, and the body more important than clothes?

Matthew 6:25

Jesus really did believe that our treasures—possessions, money, clothing, shoes, boots, coats, swimwear, hair cut, style of glasses, car, computer, iPhone and iPod and iPad and iThings and iWants and iNeeds—are sure pointers at what is most important to us. He connects our heart to our treasures. I teach these statements from Matthew 6 every semester, and not a semester goes by that I don't ask myself this question:

What do my possessions indicate about where my heart is?

Go ahead, ask yourself that same question:

What do your possessions indicate about where your heart is?

(You might want to find a quiet place to ponder this question seriously.)

● ● ● ● ●

What do your possessions reveal about
where your heart is? Are you living between two lords?

● ● ● ● ●

Jesus also knows that you have to make a choice. It is impossible, he says, to serve both God and money, and when you try serving both God and money everyone loses: you, God, and money. Instead of the real God and the real money, we get the iGod and iMoney—with a big emphasis on the "i." It's the "i" version-that-I-want of God and the "i" version-of-money-that-I-want of money, and they are seriously diminished. Living between these two competing lords means you lose both, and your own heart is diminished.

Furthermore, as we read more of his words, we see that so big was Jesus on little money that he flat-out told his followers that they didn't even need to worry about life, food, drink, or clothing. It's not because he could live without any of them. He needed to eat and drink and have clothing. No, it's because he wanted his followers to follow him into the life of being a focused follower, and if they did that they'd have the life they wanted and the food and drink and clothing they needed.

What does a focused follower look like, then? Well, there's no other way to put this: a focused follower has a heart with affections in a different direction: on the eternal, on God's kingdom, and on righteousness. Here are Jesus' words:

But store up for yourselves treasures in heaven.

Matthew 6:20

For the pagans run after all these things, and your heavenly Father knows that you need them. But seek first his kingdom and his righteousness, and all these things will be given to you as well. Therefore do not worry about tomorrow, for tomorrow will worry about itself. Each day has enough trouble of its own.

Matthew 6:32–34

There's a big reason a follower can live like this: a focused follower knows God cares; a focused follower trusts God is watching. A focused follower not only trusts that God cares and watches but the focused follower also *acts on that trust by living a life that is focused on Jesus, the kingdom, and doing God's will, and therefore lives each day knowing God will take care of what you need.* These words cry out for you to get personal and ask yourself this question:

How focused am I?

Stoics pretend life doesn't matter or they shield themselves from pain and worry, but Jesus was no stoic. Cynics vigorously and rigorously disciplined themselves to live without, but Jesus was not a cynic. Instead, Jesus comes at life's necessities from a completely different angle: he knows God as the Father, he knows this Father cares and loves his children, and he trusts and teaches his followers to trust that this loving, caring Father will look after them.

This leads us to a very important point: the first part of the Jesus Creed is to love God, and to devote one's entire heart, soul, mind, and strength to loving God. A focused follower is one who loves God. A focused follower can trust God to provide because a focused follower loves God and rests in God's love. When you rest in God's loving care, you are freed up to devote yourself to the three things Jesus focuses on in the words we quoted above: to the eternal, to the kingdom, and to God's will.

●   ●   ●   ●   ●

How do loving God and loving others
put possessions into a new perspective?

●   ●   ●   ●   ●

When Jesus tells his followers to focus on the eternal instead of on treasures that rust and can be stolen, he challenged his followers to ponder what he meant. As we read further along into Matthew 6 it becomes clear that Jesus meant "God's kingdom" and "God's righteousness." These are important words for Jews of Jesus' day, and so we want to make it clear just what Jesus wants his followers to focus on:

God's *kingdom* is the society, the gathering of people around Jesus, who strive to live out God's will in this world. God's kingdom is God's will manifested in this world among God's people.

God's *righteousness* is God's will for this world—to love God utterly and to love others utterly.

In other words, Matthew 6:33's famous "seek first his kingdom and his righteousness" describes "those who hunger and thirst for righteousness." As Jesus blessed those who hungered by telling them they'd be "filled," so he promises his focused followers this: "all these things [life, food, drink, clothing] will be given to you as well."

Perhaps you are tempted to get hyped up about these words and become a careless, happy-go-lucky, irresponsible person who doesn't work or save or live wisely and prudently, and you hope God (or your mom or your dad or your friend) bails you out while you enjoy your tranquil evenings texting your friends. This is hardly what Jesus is saying. Jesus is not talking here about "care-*less*-ness" but about "care-*free*-ness." The issue is the heart, not the hands or the feet—you are called to do what God calls you to do, and for almost one hundred percent of us that means getting a job and working hard and making money and saving and being wise. But within that life of wise work, the focused follower of Jesus strives to trust in God. Lay your heart into the safe care of God's good hands, and surrender your anxieties to God so you can focus on the eternal, the kingdom of God, and doing God's will.

We close each chapter now by reciting the Lord's Prayer. Listen to the words of this prayer as you say them and you will hear Jesus teach us about a focused following that is so focused on loving God and loving others that we are set free from worry.

Say the Lord's Prayer

CHAPTER 9

who do you think Jesus is?

● ● ● ● ●

Recite the Jesus Creed

To love God is to love Jesus and to love Jesus is to follow Jesus. If you really love God you will do whatever Jesus calls you to do.

It couldn't be simpler . . . or harder!

From the many, many occasions when Jesus must have had private encounters with wanderers and wonderers and doubters and debaters, two encounters capture the sorts of things Jesus still says to anyone who is seriously interested in the kingdom of God. Here are Jesus' words:

> When Jesus saw the crowd around him, he gave orders to cross to the other side of the lake. Then a teacher of the law came to him and said, "Teacher, I will follow you wherever you go."
> Jesus replied, "Foxes have holes and birds have nests, but the Son of Man has no place to lay his head."
>
> Another disciple said to him, "Lord, first let me go and bury my father."
> But Jesus told him, "Follow me, and let the dead bury their own dead."
>
> Matthew 8:18–22

Jesus wants followers. The rabbis in his world did too, and the rabbis said it like this: "Raise up many disciples." But Jesus did this rabbi thing in a most peculiar way, as a thoughtful reading of the words in italics shows. He seemed to hold would-be followers at arm's length until they realized what they were about to get into.

Pondering comfort

The first encounter is with a "teacher of the law," someone who might have memorized all of the Torah or at least knew all of the Torah. Not only did a teacher of the law know the Torah, but he also knew all the interpretations of the Torah. Knowledge brings power, so the teacher had plenty of status in the Jewish world. In some ways, the teachers of the law were the first century's "public intellectuals."

On that day, one religious expert risked his whole reputation. Everything he'd studied and all the honor he had achieved were put on the table when he approached Jesus and declared that he'd like to follow Jesus. Let me make this clear: it would be like your school's most vocal atheist approaching you with these words: "I want to believe in God, can you help me?"

What would you say (after your gulp and your stutters and ums and uhs and perhaps even hoping someone else would come along to help you)? My guess is that, after you got your wits about you, it might go like this: "Sure, Robin (the atheist), we meet at Griffin's house on Tuesday evenings and you are welcome to come. We've been praying for you. And, by the way, bring your Bible, but if you don't have one, we'll have one for you."

● ● ● ● ●

What would you say?

● ● ● ● ●

Jesus wasn't that encouraging. (Sorry if that makes you feel bad.)

Instead of saying, "Cool, a scribe wants us to join our group," or "Great, it's nice to see folks from the Torah group who want to follow me," Jesus digs deeper and probes further and demands even more. In essence, Jesus wants the scribe to know what he's getting into: physical hardship. The way Jesus puts it is that animals at least have a bed or a home to go to, but he is an itinerant who doesn't know where he will spend the next night or get his next meal.

The one thing that is very clear is that Jesus wants people to know what they are getting into *before they make their decision*. Following Jesus isn't like a summer retreat at a lakefront home with all sunny days and someone to drive the boat so you can ski or someone to cook so you can sleep in or someone to clean your room so you can hang all day long. It's more like being on *Survivor*. Maybe it's more like taking up a challenge to climb a mountain where you are down to one backpack, or like spending an entire summer in Africa with ineffective electricity, almost no access to the Internet, no air conditioning, lots of bugs, and folks dying from AIDS and malnutrition and lack of clean water . . . and every day rising up to greet you with big challenges to your faith. Following Jesus means loving God with everything you've got, including challenges for your body.

You might be wondering by now if Jesus expects you to do the same thing: Are we all expected to go on itinerant mission trips with no food or money? No. But the inner meaning of these lines remains firm: *Jesus wants you to ponder deeply what it means to become his follower, and he wants you to commit only if you are willing to give your entire self to him.*

Jesus is asking a simple question: Do you love me so much you will give your entire body to me?

Pondering family

The second person wanted to follow Jesus but first wanted to go home to bury his father. Once again, we are not surprised by the man's request. In the Jewish world—and in every world you and I know—burial of one's father was a first-level responsibility and a sacred act. So sacred was burial of a father that Jews were permitted to ignore going through mandatory daily prayer routines to attend to burial.

Jesus' words surely strike us as harsh: *Follow me, and let the dead bury their own dead.*

We are prone to soften this. For instance, some think the father was "spiritually dead" so the "spiritually alive" can ignore their unbelieving family. (Still seems too harsh.) Or others wonder if the would-be follower, who might be the eldest son, might be gone for up to a year since the burial of a father involved two steps: immediately the father's corpse is put into a dug-out hole in a cave or in a wall so the body can deteriorate—and I'll omit the graphic details. Then one year later the oldest son opens the burial site and checks the body to make sure it has deteriorated enough to put it in a bone box; then the body is removed and buried for good in a sacred bone box. These bone boxes are still being discovered, and you can Google them with the word *ossuary.* Perhaps this is what was going on with the man who approached Jesus, and we can see that a one-year delay might be too much delay for Jesus. But we can't be sure that Jesus was talking to an eldest son. What we've got is a very abrupt encounter between Jesus and a man who asks for a delay.

The harshness of Jesus' word strikes us, and what he said is designed to do just that: *even what we consider to be sacred is not as important as following Jesus.* That is, *even family obligations* are less important than following Jesus.

● ● ● ● ●

The harshness of Jesus' word strikes us, and what he said is designed to do just that.

● ● ● ● ●

I believe this saying emerges from a world where many families were opposing those who wanted to follow Jesus. There's another saying of Jesus that illuminates our saying. You may remember that on another occasion when Jesus said he was bringing the (metaphorical) sword of division that would (metaphorically) cut up some families, Jesus added, *your enemies will be the members of your own household* (Matthew 10:36). Jesus' brothers did not believe in Jesus at first (see John 7:1–5), and his mother at one time thought Jesus was "out of his mind" (Mark 3:21). Jesus himself learned that loving God sometimes created chaos in his own home and among his own family members.

It is very important to catch this context: Jesus isn't advocating anarchy against one's family. Jesus calls, and if one's family opposes following Jesus, Jesus says it is more important to follow him.

This brings up a difficult issue you may be facing: you may be finding the joy of knowing Jesus or the joy of wanting to follow Jesus deeply, and your parents may not think this is such a great idea. Perhaps your father or mother is an atheist; perhaps they are only nominally Christian; perhaps they are from a different denomination and think your new zeal for Jesus has jumped the shark. My advice is (1) follow Jesus first but (2) do so with loving words with your parents about how important Jesus is to you. Remember, the Jesus Creed applies to how you disagree with your parents. Your parents are wise: listen to them; but you may have to see yourself in the sketch of this man who wanted to honor his father more than follow Jesus. The latter is more important than the former.

●　●　●　●　●

Maybe you are in a similar situation—caught somewhere between Jesus and your family.

●　●　●　●　●

I know a young woman who began to follow Jesus but she was the only Christian in her house for the last two years of high school. Her parents discouraged her from attending youth group events and blocked her from attending mission trips. She had a choice at this point. One option was to convince herself that disobeying her parents to follow God was better, but it would have led to a lot more strife. Instead, she chose to obey her parents, while still honoring God as best she could. She knew that disobeying her parents was dishonoring to God and trusted that God would still bless her. He did. She now has a graduate degree from a seminary and is pursuing a career in ministry. She even has a great relationship with her parents.

If you're facing a similar situation, I hope this story will encourage you to honor God by honoring your parents and waiting to see how God uses your obedience to further his kingdom.

But remember this: Jesus' call to follow him above all remains.

Jesus' question remains the same: Do you love me more even than your family? Jesus calls us to love God with everything we've got — and that love is to be the first love of our life.

Loving within the family

Focusing on these statements of Jesus has a way of distorting family life, as if following Jesus must mean family strife. The Jesus Creed begins at home for the followers of Jesus, and when others love God and love others, the family becomes a place of safety, love, and growth. Families don't have to fight to create followers of Jesus! So it is good for us to pause here to reflect on the value of the Jesus Creed for nurturing love within the family.

I (Chris) am married to a beautiful woman named Gina. We've been married for thirteen years. I can honestly say that Gina is my best friend. Together, we have grown into deeper levels of union with God. We have come to a better understanding of ourselves by better understanding each other. We have worked hard to reframe our lives around others' needs instead of our wants, and we have become more aware every day of our role to nurture our children to love Jesus.

Part of the way we help our children see and experience loving Jesus is to find ways for them to see how much we love each other. It's the Jesus Creed. Love God—Love others. Our love for God is directly connected to our love for one another.

Here is the thing. I can't just show my kids how much I love my wife and their mom by the outer expressions of hugs and kisses. Hugs and kisses are good and all, but you can't measure love by hugs and kisses; you measure love by the virtues or the inner qualities such as commitment and presence and faithfulness and devotion. What reveals my love for Gina is my commitment to be with her, to attend to her needs, and to serve her. When my children see my commitment, they learn to see the behaviors as expressions of my commitment.

Let's look at this commitment as our inner love and our behaviors as our outer love. Followers of Jesus are changed in their "inner" and that reshapes their "outer." Jesus' radical challenge to follow him ahead of family was an outer expression of the inner reality.

The Jesus Creed, then, regulates both how we love one another within a family and how we love Jesus by following him above all. He keeps on asking the big question: Do you love me most? But behind that question is the biggest question of all:

Who is Jesus?

I don't know if you picked this up or not, but it takes some serious *chutzpah* on Jesus' part to say following him both reshapes and puts in place our family life. Listen to those words again and then think about them this way:

*Jesus is saying that following **him** . . . **him** . . . **him** . . .*
is more important than physical comfort and family.

Everyone who knows the first-century context of Jesus agrees with the following: the only thing more sacred than family is God.

Add this to what we've already considered in this chapter and here's what you get: *Jesus scandalously puts himself in the place of God for his followers.* What mattered most was following him, whether that meant revolutionizing a family into followers of Jesus or reshaping alliances within a family. Regardless, when we have finished listening to Jesus our first question comes back to this: "Who does he think he is?!"

Perhaps you have been tempted, as so many are, to think of Jesus as little more than a great teacher or a philosopher or a wise man. But C. S. Lewis long ago warned us about short-circuiting what Jesus really was claiming:

> I am trying here to prevent anyone saying the really foolish thing that people often say about Him [Jesus]: "I'm ready to accept Jesus as a great moral teacher, but I don't accept His claim to be God."

> That is the one thing we must not say. A man who was merely a man and said the sort of things Jesus said would not be a great moral teacher. He would either be a lunatic—on a level with the man who says he is a poached egg—or else he would be the Devil of Hell.

> You must make your choice. Either this man was, and is, the Son of God: or else a madman or something worse.

> You can shut Him up for a fool, you can spit at Him and kill Him as a demon; or you can fall at His feet and call Him Lord and God.

But let us not come with any patronizing nonsense about His being a great human teacher. He has not left that open to us. He did not intend to.[5]

Jesus is the Lord, and the only proper response to the Lord is to listen and to do what the Lord says. Listening to Jesus and doing what he says is what "loving God" and "loving others" are all about.

Who do you think Jesus is?

If you think he is Lord and Messiah and Savior, then the only proper response is to follow him, no matter what he asks.

● ● ● ● ●

Say the Lord's Prayer

sitting at Jesus' feet

● ● ● ● ●

Recite the Jesus Creed

My favorite high school teacher taught me German. We called him "Herr Kurr." He taught me to read German and to speak German; he taught me how to write words in a way that looked like a German did the actual writing. Most of all, Herr Kurr inspired me to dig into the German culture and into German literature, and he inspired me so much I thought I would become a missionary to Germany. Instead I became a professor, and God has used Herr Kurr in my life because I read German books all the time.

I sat at Herr Kurr's feet. I wanted to speak like him; I wanted to respond like him; I wanted to laugh at things he laughed at and I wanted to grieve over things he grieved over. He was my model and my mentor, and I was his imitator and follower. When someone criticized Herr Kurr, I defended him and showed them how they were wrong. (Like the guy who said the Spanish teacher, Mr. Diekel-something, was a better teacher. I knew that wasn't the case even though I had never sat in Mr. Diekel-something's class for even a minute.)

The one word that comes to my mind when I think how I learned from Herr Kurr is the word *posture*. And I'm not talking about whether or not I slouched in my chair in his class, but about my inner disposition toward Herr Kurr. My inner disposition was a posture that leaned toward Herr Kurr in a receptive manner. I looked up to him in order to receive wisdom from him. You could say I loved him . . . although I don't think I'd have been caught dead saying such a thing as a high school student.

● ● ● ● ●

It's all about posture.

● ● ● ● ●

The first followers of Jesus had that same posture because they loved Jesus. It's the posture of my grandson, Aksel, when his mother or father pulls out a book and he sidles up next to them and looks into the book to hear the story. It's the posture of high school athletes gathering round Mia Hamm or Maya Moore or Coach K or Albert Pujols as they share their wisdom and stories about how to play the game. It's the posture of the English students who want to become writers when they meet their first novelist at a local bookstore.

Sitting at Jesus' feet

You can't read this story from Luke 10:38–42 (NRSV) without imagining the details:

> *Now as they went on their way, he entered a certain village,*
> *where a woman named Martha welcomed him into her*
> *home.*

We don't know much about Martha, but the church will eventually turn her into a stereotype the way novelists like Harper Lee stereotype characters — like Scout and Atticus. As we read this story about Jesus we will begin to turn away from Ms. Distraction (Martha) toward Ms. Devotion (Martha's sister, Mary):

> *She had a sister named Mary, who sat at the Lord's feet and*
> *listened to what he was saying.*

Mary's got the posture; Martha's got the problem. We all know people like both of them.

● ● ● ● ●

Mary's got the posture;
Martha's got the problem.

● ● ● ● ●

But Martha was distracted by her many tasks; so she came to him and asked, "Lord, do you not care that my sister has left me to do all the work by myself? Tell her then to help me."

As if Jesus is going to coax Mary out of the posture of a disciple to become a fussy kitchen worker like Ms. Distraction. . . .

But the Lord answered her, "Martha, Martha, you are worried and distracted by many things; there is need of only one thing. Mary has chosen the better part, which will not be taken away from her."

Martha flits; Mary sits. Martha worries about many things; Mary wonders about one thing. Martha stares into a pot; Mary gazes into the eyes of Jesus.

What Martha (Stewart!) is doing here is caring more about the doilies in the dining room than the Lord in the living room. It would be like having Luciano Pavarotti, who was the world's greatest opera singer before his death, stop by for a visit. He rings the doorbell and asks if he might be able to perform an aria for you. And while everyone gathers around to listen and enjoy the singing, you stay in the kitchen to make a nice appetizer.

Now, there's nothing wrong with a tasty artichoke dip, but you're missing the point. If Pavarotti is in your house, you should stop everything you're doing to listen to him, to enjoy his singing. Similarly, Jesus calls us to himself not just to serve him, but to sit at his feet first—to take the posture that Mary took, to learn from him, and to worship him.

Mary loves Jesus.

Martha loves working more than loving Jesus.

The Jesus Creed was practiced by Mary.

The Jesus Creed was subverted by Martha.

Go back and read through the italicized text above and underline the word *Lord*. Connect that word *Lord* with the posture of Mary: sitting at the feet of one's rabbi, which means "my master/teacher," was to assume the posture of someone who saw the teacher as Lord. A later statement by a rabbi illustrates our point: "Make your house be a meeting-house for the Sages, and sit in the dust of their feet and drink in their words with thirst."[6]

If Jesus is the Lord, then the proper posture we are to have is to "sit at his feet" and "listen" to him.

The invitation

Jesus, who is Lord, expected everyone who followed him to sit at his feet, and there's an incredibly emotional story about this in the Gospels. Mary, mother of Jesus and the one who knew from an angel that God was going to make Jesus the Messiah of Israel, which means king . . . anyway, Mary heard reports about Jesus' behaviors and people's reactions to him that made her think that Jesus was going to get himself killed if he didn't stop hanging with the wrong people and getting all the right people mad at him. So she marched down with her kids to Capernaum to fetch Jesus and save him from himself. (You can read this in Mark 3:21 and 3:31.)

So they got to Capernaum, knocked on the door (probably Peter's), and the person at the door went inside the place to tell Jesus his mother and family were outside. Jesus' next words were and are stunning:

"Who are my mother and my brothers?" he asked. Then
he looked at those seated in a circle around him and said,
"Here are my mother and my brothers! Whoever does God's
will is my brother and sister and mother."

Mark 3:33–35

It doesn't matter if Mary talked with angels; it doesn't matter if Mary is the mother of the Messiah; it doesn't matter if everyone in history will call her "blessed." What matters is one thing: What's her posture? or, Does she sit at Jesus' feet and listen to him?

Even Jesus' mother had to learn that her son was the Lord. The only way to be properly postured before her son was to sit at his feet with the others and listen to Jesus.

So what can we do to learn this posture?

What's your posture?

Jesus isn't here the way he was then, but he's still with us in the Gospels and in the fellowship of the saints, and he abides with us in the church, which is the body of Christ. So, let me suggest that we can learn this posture first by soaking ourselves in the story of Jesus. We can do this by reading the Gospels, reading them slowly and reading them often, and then reading how his closest followers — the apostles — carried on the witness of Jesus to their generations. We can then ponder the apostolic writings such as the letters of Paul and Peter and John. My suggestion: begin every day, or end every day, or take some time in every day, by sitting at Jesus' feet through reading the Gospels. Start with Mark or John, then read Luke or Matthew. Read them slowly; read them often. Ask yourself throughout the day, "What would Jesus say about this?" If you soak yourself in Jesus' teachings and life, you'll soon find you have answers to that question.

● ● ● ● ●

What can we do to learn the posture?

● ● ● ● ●

Gather with other followers of Jesus, pray with them and read the Bible with them, and listen to the Spirit speak to you through them.

But let me add one more point: posture is what matters. Gathering to learn, gathering to gain new information, gathering to feel like you are doing the right thing, gathering to be with your friends who are part of your Bible-reading group, or even loving the bustle of the gathering—and, yes, gathering to feel spiritual . . . these are not enough. They lead to "branding" ourselves.

No, the proper posture is the Jesus-Creed soaked posture of Mary: it is a posture of loving God by sitting at the feet of Jesus *in order to hear life-giving and life-transforming words from Jesus*. So, before you gather and as you gather, ask God to make you receptive to the words of Jesus so that you can, like Mary, find the "better part." Jesus promises her and he promises you the same thing: the better part (of being with Jesus) "will not be taken away."

● ● ● ● ●

Say the Lord's Prayer

you are Jesus (seriously.)

● ● ● ● ●

Recite the Jesus Creed

"Connect the Dots" books contain pictures that appear only after you have connected the dots with lines. I loved these as a kid, but my problem was that I connected the dots and finished the book as quickly as possible because I wanted to see what the pictures were.

There are dots to connect in the story of Jesus in the Gospels.

I want to connect four dots in the Gospel of Matthew. These dots, once connected, can open our eyes to what our task in this world is. The image that will appear once we get these four dots connected amazes me even though I've taught this dozens of times and thought it about hundreds of times more. The four dots are four statements made by Jesus: Matthew 4:23, Matthew 9:35, Matthew 10:1, and Matthew 10:40. I want now to print out these verses so you can see the "dots," draw lines between them, and see if you see what I see.

Dot 1

Jesus went throughout Galilee, teaching in their synagogues and proclaiming the good news of the kingdom and *curing every disease and every sickness* among the people.

NRSV

Dot 2

Then Jesus went about all the cities and villages, teaching in their synagogues, and proclaiming the good news of the kingdom, and *curing every disease and every sickness*.   NRSV

Dot 3

Then Jesus summoned his twelve disciples and gave them authority over unclean spirits, to cast them out, and to *cure every disease and every sickness*.   NRSV

Dot 4

Whoever welcomes you welcomes me, and whoever welcomes me welcomes the one who sent me.   NRSV

I cheated a bit and added emphasis to these quotations to make this easier: in Dot 1 and Dot 2 Matthew describes the ministry of Jesus: he teaches, he proclaims, and he cures. If you have time, you can read Matthew 5:1–9:34 because in those chapters Matthew illustrates each of those three elements in Jesus' ministry.

Then (Dot 3) Matthew tells us that Jesus sent the twelve to extend the mission of Jesus, and Matthew makes this very explicit: he uses the identical words—and this is the only place in the whole Bible these words are used—for the disciples' ministry as the words used for Jesus' ministry: "to cure every disease and every sickness." Identical words. What Jesus does, disciples are to do.

But it is Dot 4 that creates the full image for the other three.

> Jesus has a ministry (Dots 1 and 2).
> He empowers his followers to do the same ministry (Dot 3).

And then Jesus tells his disciples that *how people respond to them is their response to Jesus*. In other words, the follower of Jesus not only represents Jesus to others; the follower of Jesus *is the presence of Jesus to others!*

The disciples represent Jesus (Dot 4).

This, too, is very Jewish. There's an old rabbinic statement that says, "the one who is sent is the one who sent him." (You might translate it this way to make it clearer: "the one who is sent *IS* the one who sent him.")

We. Are. Jesus

Yes, this is a Wow! Take a moment to read it slowly enough to take it all in. We are Jesus, and this is exactly why the great apostle Paul constantly referred to churches as the "body of Christ." Here are some of Paul's choice words:

> *For just as the body is one and has many members, and all the members of the body, though many, are one body, so it is with Christ. For in the one Spirit we were all baptized into one body—Jews or Greeks, slaves or free—and we were all made to drink of one Spirit.*
>
> 1 Corinthians 12:12–13, NRSV

Perhaps you are like me and grew up with these words, and they are "whatever!" or "ho hum" kinds of words. Not so with those first readers of Paul's letters. They were "You've-got-to-be-kiddin'-me!" and "LOL!" kinds of words. As the first Christians heard those words of Paul in Corinth they would have dropped their jaws and wondered aloud at the privilege— and sacred responsibility—they now had (and were!). We are the body of Christ; we are his body; we represent him now . . . on earth.

It's weird, if you're honest, to believe these words. So, we've got to emphasize this: We—you and I, you and your family, you and others in your Bible study, you and your church, or you and your Christian friends— you and we and all of us are the very body of Christ. We (together and not just alone) represent Christ. We are what others see of Christ.

But let's get personal with this.

You. Are. Jesus

- You love Jesus most by being Jesus' agent.
- The best way to do this is to live the Jesus Creed daily.
- You represent Jesus everywhere you go.
- Everyone who sees you is seeing Jesus.

Jesus has given you the responsibility to show him to others, and to reveal to others what he's like, and to observe what he can do and is doing in this world.

● ● ● ● ●

Wouldn't you rather that this not be true?

● ● ● ● ●

Tell me the truth: Wouldn't you rather that this *not* be true? I know I would (often). When I'm at my best—cooking for my wife or calling my children or helping a neighbor or serving at church or mentoring a student in my office, when these things are happening I don't mind thinking about this. But when I'm tired and cranky, when I'm behind on some assignment, or when I'm in traffic and need to get home, or when some dipstick ahead of me on the golf course is chatting and not putting out or keeping the appropriate pace . . . that's when I'd rather these words of Jesus not be true. I'd rather not be Jesus' personal representative in those moments; I'd rather be a jerk. (And sometimes I am.) I'd rather Jesus' clear words not be so clear.

But they are always true.

Still, there's some realistic grace here too.

The apostle Paul wrote words that will both knock us off the high pedestal and remind us that, yes, God works with us just as we are. The apostle

calls us "clay pots," and it might first offend you, but think about it a bit and
you'll realize that being a clay pot is an image of God's goodness to us:

> *But we have this treasure in clay jars, so that it may be*
> *made clear that this extraordinary power belongs to God*
> *and does not come from us.*
>
> 2 Corinthians 4:7, NRSV

We are clay jars (or pots), and surely you've seen some of these in art
class or perhaps in the garden. Plants often come in clay pots. What this
means is that we are ordinary, we are breakable, and we are not gorgeous
(he didn't say a picturesque vase or a marble statue—and he knew what
such things looked like because they were all over the Roman Empire).
Instead, Paul wants us to know we are ordinary. And ordinary is OK. We
love God when we realize we are his clay pots and when we let God's
grace turn our clay pot into an instrument of love.

●　●　●　●　●

Ordinary is OK.

●　●　●　●　●

Why? So when God works through us it will be really clear that it was
God who was doing the work. We are so tempted to take all the credit and
to stand around after doing something compassionate until someone says,
"You are so helpful. You are so compassionate. I admire you." We are
tempted to work so hard so we can be so good . . . and we forget that our
hard work is sometimes what others praise.

But not Paul. He wants people to say, "God was at work in you [you
clay pot!]." A friend of mine, a pastor in South Africa in the heart of one
of Johannesburg's most famous townships, Soweto, started a church—and
the name of the church? Kleypot. (South African for "clay pot.") Why did
he call the church that? Because its members knew they were ordinary

Christians—clay pot sorts—who were filled with God's amazing grace, and that it was God's grace that was turning clay pots into vessels of transformation.

The best news I have to tell you is this:

You are Jesus.
You are Jesus *as a clay pot.*

God wants to be the presence of Jesus in you, just as you are, broken and not always on your best game, sinning and asking forgiveness, sometimes immature but knowing better . . . and even when you aren't all together, God wants to use you and show that God's grace is at work *even when the cracks in your clay plot are visible to everyone.*

Have you ever heard or read these words?

"Christ has no body now on earth but yours;
yours are the only hands with which he can do his work,
yours are the only feet with which he can go about this world,
yours are the only eyes through which his compassion can shine forth
upon a troubled world.

Christ has no body now on earth but yours."

These are memorable words from Teresa of Avila.

You are Jesus. Seriously.

Say the Lord's Prayer

be a boundary breaker

● ● ● ● ●

Recite the Jesus Creed

In many ways Erika was ordinary but her sensitivity was more than ordinary. She was a college student at North Park University when she noticed that too many kids from local grade and middle and high schools were going home alone. She wanted to do something about it . . . but what's a student to do? She had no money, and then she had papers and quizzes and assignments and reading and reading and reading . . . and not that much time . . . and who knows if anyone would help? And will the school get behind the project?

So she stuck her neck out, asked around, and *After Hours* was created: a room and a safe place for school kids to go after school. They could get something to eat, have some young adult attention, and also get a little tutoring. Before long *After Hours* caught on and the President (of the USA) at the time awarded the program something like $150,000. Ten years or more later, it's still going, and more and more of our students have caught on to the concept that ministry can begin in college and it can begin in the campus's neighborhood.

● ● ● ● ●

Are you waiting until later
to do ministry?
Ministry can begin now.

● ● ● ● ●

I will tell you what I like about what Erika did: she was a Jesus Creed young woman, she acted to meet the needs she saw, and she had the courage to stick it out. There were some who probably thought she was wasting her time and some of the school's money, but she saw a need and acted on it with courage. I see Erika as one of the North Park students who broke through a boundary—the boundary of becoming too fixated on one's school assignments or thinking that ministry is what happens during the summer or over spring break. Or, maybe you think real ministry is far away in some godforsaken place in Africa or Haiti or Argentina. It's not a little ironic that Erika's boundary breaking occurred just outside her campus dorm.

Jesus the boundary breaker

We all, you included, need to rethink this from the top down and from the bottom up: ministry doesn't begin later, and it doesn't begin somewhere else. It begins now, with you and your neighbor. Jesus Creed people reach out in love to those who need it—and those who need it are around you, in the room next to you, and in your neighborhood.

But ministry doesn't mean glow and glory.

Everywhere Jesus went someone got offended. Jesus was the Original Boundary Breaking Machine. Jesus even got his followers in trouble because they were implicated in everything he did. Boundary breakers, like Erika, enter into an unknown territory, and sometimes it's enemy territory. Boundary breakers open new paths for others to follow. They create space for God's fresh grace. Boundary breakers know loving God and loving others matters more than anything else.

Those who are most offended by boundary breakers are those with the most to lose. When boundary breakers break through, someone is provoked; it goes with new territory.

In three successive episodes in the Gospels, found in Matthew 9:1–17, Jesus breaks down boundaries and offends the religious leaders. In the first, Jesus offers *forgiveness* to a paralyzed man and then heals him to make his point very clear, and the teachers of the law find Jesus theologically wrong. In the second, Jesus offers *fellowship* to a tax collector, who was too connected to Rome and its idolatrous ways, and the Pharisees think Jesus is flaunting Jewish law by eating with sinners. In the third, Jesus offers *freedom* to suspend fasting while Jesus, the messianic King, is with them, but the disciples of John and the Pharisees team up to question Jesus' commitment to God.

● ● ● ● ●

> Three words for a boundary breaker:
> *forgiveness, fellowship,*
> and *freedom.*

● ● ● ● ●

These three words, *forgiveness—fellowship—freedom*, are three of the most important words to describe what Jesus was doing. They are probably the three most important words a boundary breaker experiences, and I know Erika experienced each. She was seeking through fellowship to create a new freedom for local kids and through it all the forgiveness of God was seen and offered.

What is often unobserved is that each of these three words is shaped by Jesus' love of God and love of others. Jesus extended forgiveness (and healing) to a paralyzed man because he loved him and because out of that love he wanted to do something for the man. Jesus opened the doors of fellowship to a despised tax collector because God loved tax collectors and Jesus wanted that man to be restored to God and to the others in the Jewish world. And Jesus suspended fasting while he was around because he knew that God's love was being showered upon the world so heavily that it was time to *feast* and not *fast*.

Suggestions

I have a few suggestions for you, and they are all based on one simple idea: if we love God and love others, which means that we are to follow Jesus as his personal representatives, and if Jesus is one who offers forgiveness and fellowship and freedom, then we are called

- to be people who offer forgiveness,
- to be people who open the door of fellowship
- and to be people who create freedom for others.

Erika did just those things.

● ● ● ● ●

What can you do, right now, this month, this year?

● ● ● ● ●

What can you do to be a personal agent of forgiveness and fellowship and freedom?

Let me begin with what I think is the hardest: Who in your life are you struggling to forgive? Jesus calls you to be an agent of forgiveness. Who in your life do you think has been beaten down by not being forgiven? Do you know people in your school or church or family or neighborhood who have been rejected? Do they need to experience the grace of God's forgiveness? What can you do—concretely—to be an agent of forgiveness?

● ● ● ● ●

Forgiveness and fellowship always create freedom.

● ● ● ● ●

My suggestion is simple: *invite them into your fellowship.* I don't know what your fellowship looks like, but I suspect it's a small group of friends, or it's a youth group at your church. I urge you to consider inviting someone who is rejected (the paralyzed man was not accepted in society and the tax collector was seen as the scum of the earth) into your fellowship. Tell everyone (without posing, without branding) in your group what you are doing, why you are doing this, and then tell them there's going to be one rule: let the fellowship flow by being friendly and loving and gracious.

At this point, you may be feeling a little uncomfortable. "I have my group of friends, and I've worked very hard to get them and to keep them. I like everything the way it is," you might be saying. I understand, but I want to challenge you that Jesus did things differently. One of the most difficult passages for me to obey is found (once again) in the Sermon on the Mount, where Jesus sees through our tendency to want to be rewarded for doing easy things. In Matthew 5:46–47, Jesus says: "If you love those who love you, what reward will you get? Are not even the tax collectors doing that? And if you greet only your own people, what are you doing more than others?" Sometimes we feel really good about ourselves when we're nice to people who are like us. "Look at me being such a good Christian!" we think. But Jesus' point is: how is that *any different* from anyone else you meet? *Everyone's* nice to their friends. But *you* must be nice, Jesus is saying—no getting around this one!— to the nasty and the rude and the forgotten. That's what being a boundary breaker is all about.

What will surprise you is what happens next: when we break boundaries because we forgive others or extend forgiveness to others or invite others into our fellowship, *freedom is created.* Every time. World without end. Forgiveness and fellowship *always generate that Holy Spirit kind of freedom.*

The apostle Paul, in 2 Corinthians 3:17, says that "where the Spirit of the Lord is, there is freedom." And when we tap into the Spirit's power to break boundaries, the same Spirit unleashes a kind of freedom in the world that is other-worldly.

I don't mean that wild kind of party freedom, which really isn't freedom (it's recklessness).

I mean that kind of soul-expanding, heart-pumping, friendship-creating, and hope-generating freedom of knowing that God's love transforms, that loving God and loving others is the path we are made to travel, and that when we love others genuinely, forgiveness and fellowship and freedom flow like a river.

● ● ● ● ●

Say the Lord's Prayer

now what?

The whole point of *The Jesus Creed for Students* is to present to you what we think is the most revolutionary moral vision ever given to humans in history. Much of what we have pondered comes from the Sermon on the Mount, the most famous sermon in history. But what we have observed is that much of that sermon emerges from the Jesus Creed. At the rock bottom of all ethical reality for anyone who takes following Jesus seriously is the twofold duty, the twofold command. That duty or command is to love God with everything you've got and to love others the way you love yourself.

You can change your life and you can influence your world if you will repeat daily the Jesus Creed and then, not just repeat it, but put the Jesus Creed into practice. You will become a boundary breaker simply by living the Jesus Creed.

So let me encourage you one more time: when you get up and when you go to bed, wherever you are and no matter what your day was like, say the Jesus Creed and then say the Lord's Prayer too. Over time you will see the wisdom of God and the wisdom of Jesus, who gave these to us so we would know how to live the radical vision of the kingdom of God.

the Jesus Creed—do it

Hear O Israel:
The Lord our God, the Lord is One.
Love the Lord your God with all your heart,
With all your soul,
With all your mind,
And with all your strength.

The second is this:

Love your neighbor as yourself.
There is no commandment greater than these.

(From Mark 12:29–31)

the Lord's Prayer

Our Father who art in heaven,
Hallowed be thy name.

Thy kingdom come,
Thy will be done on earth as it is in heaven.

Give us this day our daily bread.

Forgive us our sins as we forgive those who sin against us.

And lead us not into temptation.
But deliver us from evil.

For thine is the kingdom,
The power,
And the glory.
Forever and ever.
Amen.

about Scot, Chris, and Syler

Scot McKnight

is an authority on the New Testament, early Christianity, and the historical Jesus. He is the Karl A. Olsson Professor in Religious Studies at North Park University in Chicago, Illinois. A popular teacher and speaker, Dr. McKnight has been interviewed on radio and television, and is regularly asked to teach the Jesus Creed in churches around the USA and in many other countries. Scot is the author of more than thirty books, including scholarly works, commentaries, and the award-winning book for all Christians *The Jesus Creed: Loving God, Loving Others* (Paraclete, 2004).

His blog, Jesus Creed, has been rated by Technorati.com as one of the top-trafficked Christian blogs in the world (http://www.patheos.com/community/jesuscreed). Scot and his wife, Kristen, live in Libertyville, Illinois, where they are long-suffering Cubs fans and also enjoy traveling, gardening, and cooking. They have two adult children and one grandchild (so far).

Chris Folmsbee

is the director of Barefoot Ministries, a nonprofit youth ministry training and publishing company in Kansas City. He is the author of several books, most recently *Story, Signs, and Sacred Rhythms: A Narrative Approach to Youth Ministry* (Zondervan, 2011). Chris's blog is at www.anewkindofyouthministry.com. He is married to Gina and they have three incredible kids.

Syler Thomas

has been the High School Pastor at Christ Church in Lake Forest, Illinois, for twelve years. A native Texan, he's a graduate of DePaul University and Trinity Evangelical Divinity School. He is the coauthor of *Game Plan*, a book for graduating high school seniors, and writes a column for *Youthworker Journal*. His blog is at www.syberspace.typepad.com. He is married to Heidi, and they have four wonderful children.

You can reach all three of them at:

Jesus Creed Students

Paraclete Press

P.O. Box 1568

Orleans, MA 02653

E-mail: JesusCreedStudents@paracletepress.com

notes

1. This story can be found in the Babylonian Talmud, the anthology of Jewish lore and interpretation. The specific book is called *Moed: Shabbath* 31a. I have paraphrased slightly the translation found in I. Epstein, *The Babylonian Talmud* (London: Soncino, 1938), 4.1.140.

2. See J. P. Moreland, *The Lost Virtue of Happiness* (Colorado Springs: NavPress, 2006), 17–18.

3. C. S. Lewis, *Mere Christianity* (New York: Macmillan, 1956), 89, opening up his chapter called "Forgiveness."

4. We recommend Shane Claiborne's *The Irresistible Revolution* (Grand Rapids, MI: Zondervan, 2006).

5. C. S. Lewis, *Mere Christianity* (New York: Macmillan, 1956), 40–41. Since there are a number of editions of this book, I point out that you can find this quote in the last paragraph of the chapter called "The Shocking Alternative."

6. My paraphrase of Mishnah Abot 1.4.

about paraclete press

Who We Are

Paraclete Press is a publisher of books, recordings, and DVDs on Christian spirituality. Our publishing represents a full expression of Christian belief and practice—from Catholic to Evangelical, from Protestant to Orthodox.

We are the publishing arm of the Community of Jesus, an ecumenical monastic community in the Benedictine tradition. As such, we are uniquely positioned in the marketplace without connection to a large corporation and with informal relationships to many branches and denominations of faith.

What We Are Doing

Books

Paraclete publishes books that show the richness and depth of what it means to be Christian. Although Benedictine spirituality is at the heart of all that we do, we publish books that reflect the Christian experience across many cultures, time periods, and houses of worship. We publish books that nourish the vibrant life of the church and its people—books about spiritual practice, formation, history, ideas, and customs.

We have several different series, including the best-selling Paraclete Essentials and Paraclete Giants series of classic texts in contemporary English; A Voice from the Monastery—men and women monastics writing about living a spiritual life today; award-winning literary faith fiction and poetry; and the Active Prayer Series that brings creativity and liveliness to any life of prayer.

Recordings

From Gregorian chant to contemporary American choral works, our music recordings celebrate sacred choral music through the centuries. Paraclete distributes the recordings of the internationally acclaimed choir Gloriæ Dei Cantores, praised for their "rapt and fathomless spiritual intensity" by *American Record Guide*, and the Gloriæ Dei Cantores Schola, which specializes in the study and performance of Gregorian chant. Paraclete is also the exclusive North American distributor of the recordings of the Monastic Choir of St. Peter's Abbey in Solesmes, France, long considered to be a leading authority on Gregorian chant.

DVDs

Our DVDs offer spiritual help, healing, and biblical guidance for life issues: grief and loss, marriage, forgiveness, anger management, facing death, and spiritual formation.

Learn more about us at our website:
www.paracletepress.com, or call us toll-free at 1-800-451-5006.

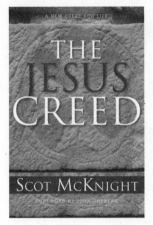

The Jesus Creed
Loving God, Loving Others

Scot McKnight

978-1-55725-400-9
Paperback, $16.99

Love God with all your heart, soul, mind, and strength, but also love others as yourselves. Discover how the Jesus Creed of love for God and others can transform your life.

Winner of
the 2005
Christianity Today
Book Award

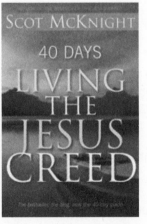

40 Days Living the Jesus Creed

Scot McKnight

978-1-55725-577-8
Paperback, $14.95

"Scot McKnight stirs the treasures of our Lord's life in an engaging fashion. He did so with *The Jesus Creed*, and does so again with *40 Days Living the Jesus Creed*. Make sure this new guide for living is on your shelf." —Max Lucado

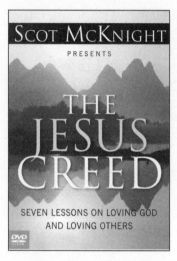